THE SECRET LIFE
OF
SOOTY

GEOFF TIBBALLS

RINGPRESS

RINGPRESS

An imprint of Ringpress Ltd.,
Spirella House, Letchworth,
Hertfordshire SG6 4ET

© Geoff Tibballs and Ringpress Books
1990

First published 1990

ISBN: 0 948955 56 2

Production consultants: Landmark Ltd.
Typeset by Ringpress Books
Printed in Great Britain by Cox & Wyman Ltd, Reading, Berks

CONTENTS

ACKNOWLEDGEMENTS

My thanks go to the entire Corbett family and friends for their time and patience, to Matthew's secretary Heather and to the World and Sooty Museum in Shipley, Yorkshire.

Geoff Tibballs
Summer 1990

FOREWORD

Sooty symbolises the speed at which I wish the world was still turning. Harry Corbett created him in a time when life was less complicated, less competitive and certainly, in media terms, much less violent.

Harry Corbett kept the routine simple and, with a very intriguing Northern cunning (in the best sense of the word) engaged our attention with a basic music-hall routine with himself as the straight man and the n̄ ighty Sooty (and side-kick Sweep) as the mischief makers. Let's face it, it's pretty corny stuff. Yet . . . Sooty is a subtle character who, if you missed him in your childhood, you may discover as an adult with your own child, as I did with my son Dhani.

The experience of watching *The Sooty Show* with a toddler on your lap embraces tender moments to be greatly valued in this mad world. And the Sooty experience continues to sustain real survival of childhood innocence, a safe haven from the bombardment of today's aggressive entertainment for children.

The early days of Sooty were played out in those thrilling, flickering black and white "snowstorm" television sets, and it is a tribute to Matthew Corbett that decades later the great Corbett creation still lives , although the mighty Harry has moved on to join the Great Majority. Matthew (guaranteed, in the words of Eric Idle, to break the ice at any party) perhaps himself doesn't realise what an achievement it is to be able to capture the hearts of young ones with a little glove hero in this high-tech, animated world that screams at our children to watch and buy.

Sooty is proof that sanity is still with us. Good luck for the future.

George Harrison

INTRODUCTION

When I sat down to write this book, I instantly became aware of the difficulties encountered by the biographers of Sinatra, Dietrich and Garbo. How can a mere mortal do justice to the career of a living legend? For make no mistake, Sooty is a living legend. He qualifies on both counts. Firstly, he is still going strong on this the fortieth anniversary of his first major performance and he is arguably more popular than ever, having recently achieved international celebrity status. He is now a major star Down Under. Australia gave us Kylie and Jason and we returned the compliment with a puppet of our own, Sooty. Secondly, there cannot be a person in Britain who has not heard of him. Not even Bros can claim that. Now at the ripe old age of forty-two, Sooty has outlived such luminaries as James Dean, Henry V, Marilyn Monroe, Rudolph Valentino and Alexander the Great. Yet he looks younger than ever, a glowing illustration of the virtues of clean-living.

Sooty's distinguished career has already spanned ten British Prime Ministers and he has mixed with royalty, lords of the realm, pop stars and been interviewed by Terry Wogan. What more is there to life?

Yet throughout everything Sooty has maintained the sort of silence that made Howard Hughes seem like a publicity-seeker. Cynics will say that this is because he can't speak, even pointing out that he hasn't got a mouth as such. But the truth is that Sooty has always preferred to keep a low profile. Back in the Sixties, did you ever see Sooty at the head of an anti-Vietnam War demonstration? Did Harry Corbett ever emulate John

Lennon and claim that Sooty was more popular than Jesus? Of course not. That simply isn't Sooty's style.

In the circumstances it was with some trepidation that I set about obtaining the first-ever in-depth interview with Sooty, not one where he merely drones on about his new aerobics tapes or plugs his latest book. What devastating revelations would he come up with about his private life? What was his role in the Profumo affair? Was it true about him and Fiona Wright?

Above all, I wanted to know the dark secrets about his intimate relationship with the Corbetts. After a particularly violent studio altercation with the hammer and water-pistol, did Harry ever bully Sooty when he got him home? Did he exact his revenge by using Sooty to wipe the dinner dishes? Was Matthew's hand any warmer? And with showbusiness circles full of stories about double acts that didn't really get on together, did Sooty and Sweep socialise much off-screen or was there profound professional jealousy between the two? And is it true that Soo once ditched Sooty for one of the Wombles?

Alas, we'll never know. For while Harry and Matthew Corbett were only too happy to talk, Sooty remained steadfastly silent. Whether his press agent had advised him against doing the interview I can only speculate. I have heard that he once had a bad experience with the *News of the World*. But throughout my interviews he just sat there slumped in a corner, head bowed, looking as if he'd seen one Tequila Sunrise too many.

As I say, fortunately the entire Corbett family were infinitely more communicative and were prepared to tell all about Sooty's hitherto undisclosed life of sex, drugs and rock 'n' roll. I appreciate that this will come as a devastating shock, but sadly there is unequivocal evidence that behind that clean-cut image, he has had more than a few brushes with the seamier side of society. There's no question about it, Sooty has lived life in the fast lane, not the bus lane. But I feel that even though it is akin to revealing that the mighty Champion the Wonder Horse was really just two Shetland Ponies stitched together or that Lassie can't even master the most basic word processor, this is a story that has to be told.

For me, meeting the late Harry Corbett was like the fulfilment of a childhood dream. As a youngster in the innocent days of the Fifties when an Acid Party meant sharing your Spangles, Sooty was my undoubted hero. Older boys worshipped comic supermen like Dan Dare, The Black Sapper and Roy of the Rovers but with a wave of his magic wand, a quick sprinkle of oofle dust and a burst of "Izzy Whizzy, Let's Get Busy", Sooty could wipe them all off the face of the Earth. Like millions of children, I never missed his antics, which brightened up Sunday afternoons after hours of Vera Lynn requests on *Two-Way Family Favourites*. An episode that I particularly remember was one I watched with my equally enthralled grandmother and where Sooty tried to cook a chicken. When I relayed this (no pun intended) to Harry, to my amazement he had instant recall of the programme, together with title and plot. Here was a man who evidently loved every minute of his work.

Harry Corbett was a big star at that time, right up there at the top alongside the likes of Billy Cotton, Liberace and Armand and Michaela Denis. The Sooty theme music was as instantly recognisable as the National Anthem and, as his fame spread, he was sold overseas to places like France, Canada and Scandinavia and even dubbed in German. Vorsprung Durch Sooty!

The incredible aspect about the whole Sooty saga is that while other children's characters have fallen by the wayside, he has managed to retain his enormous popularity, even though behind the scenes there have been moments of profound heartache for the Corbetts. Audience records are currently being broken all over the country as, even by his own high standards, Sooty enjoys something of a renaissance. More and more children (and adults) than ever before are flocking to see his stage shows, a tribute not only to Harry's creation but also to the way in which his son Matthew has been able to maintain and increase the momentum. My own daughters, Nicola and Lindsey, enjoy the programmes every bit as much as I used to. I didn't have to nail them down to the carpet and force them to watch Sooty just because I was writing a book about him. I never had to resort to the ultimate threat and say: "If you don't watch Sooty, I'll make you stay up late and watch Jeremy Beadle. . . " Quite simply, Sooty is the one character who has managed to exercise a uniform appeal over four generations with vastly different tastes. And as many adults will testify after a glass or two of Chablis, you never really grow out of Sooty.

My only regret is that Harry didn't live to see the completion of this book. Sadly he died last year, ultimately the result of the stress and strain accumulated over all those years of racing around the country and thinking up new ideas for Sooty, the puppet he adored. Although the immense amount of hard work involved caused both Harry and his devoted wife Marjorie considerable pain, they derived as much pleasure from Sooty as did any child. To them, Sooty wasn't a puppet, he was a son. In his life, Harry brought so much to so many. For millions of people when Harry Corbett died, a part of their childhood died too. But thanks to the efforts of Matthew over the past fourteen years, it is likely that Sooty will carry on regardless through the Nineties and probably well into the twenty-first century. Man may colonise the Moon, we may all live in solar-heated houses, the Channel Tunnel might even by completed, but Sooty will still be conducting choruses of "Izzy Whizzy, Let's Get Busy".

Because of his vow of silence, it seems the world is destined never to know exactly what Sooty thought of Harry Corbett but I'm sure if he had spoken, he would have wanted to thank Harry profusely. . . if only for keeping his finger nails short.

CHAPTER ONE

IN THE BEGINNING

It was July 1948. Clement Attlee was Prime Minister, the National Health Service had just been created, Britain was in the grip of rationing and Bradford engineer and part-time magician Harry Corbett was on holiday in Blackpool with his wife Marjorie and sons David, three, and Peter four months. It was a miserable week. The weather was dismal, a remark that could also be applied to Mrs. Haddock's boarding house where the family were staying. Mrs. Haddock didn't live up to her surname's culinary connotations and took rationing to extremes, leaving the Corbetts so hungry that they had to sneak out after meal-times to fill up. "We were half-starved all week," confessed Harry. "I honestly don't know how we survived. Needless to say, we all caught colds — in fact instead of spending our money on entertainment, we spent most of it at the chemist's. Not surprisingly, the kids were well and truly fed up. It looked like being a holiday to remember all right, but for all the wrong reasons."

The days were dragging by, so to pass the time Harry took David on a tram ride one afternoon and they braved the elements long enough to venture on to the beach. "I was determined we should go on the beach at least once," continued Harry. "We had David's bucket and spade and we stuck it out for an hour, although it seemed like an eternity. I think we were the only two there. Even the donkeys stayed indoors that week."

On the way back, the windswept pair passed North Pier, on the end of which were a few novelty and joke shops. In the window of one shop, which still stands to this day, Harry spotted a glove puppet teddy bear, price 7s 6d, propped up against a pair of roller skates. He later learned that it had been made by an old lady on the pier. "I'd always had a thing about teddy bears," said Harry, "and this one had a cheeky face. It was almost as if it was saying 'don't leave me here, come and get me.' I went back to the digs and kept on about it to Marjorie. She said: 'If it's made such an impression on you, stop wittering and go back and buy it.'" So Harry returned to the shop and brought the teddy bear back to Mrs. Haddock's in a brown paper bag. When Marjorie first saw the prized purchase, she thought it looked a bit like a rat. But that "rat" developed into a cuddly character that has enchanted millions and become the world's most famous glove puppet as well as a national institution — Sooty.

The Sooty story really begins ten months before the end of the First World War on 28 January, 1918 when Harry Corbett was born at 21, Edmund St. , Bradford, a terraced house situated just a few hundred yards from the city's famous Alhambra Theatre. His parents used to take him to the Alhambra every Thursday evening for the first house. To young Harry, it was an awe-inspiring place and not for a moment did he think that he'd one day be appearing on stage there. Harry's father Jim had been a miner, but when he had married Florence Ramsden, he had also married into the fish and chip shop business because Florence's brother, and therefore Harry's uncle, was none other than that doyen of battered plaice, Harry Ramsden. When it came to fish and chips, Ramsden was The Codfather.

The Corbetts proceeded to run a fish and chip shop in Bradford. Meanwhile Harry Ramsden was doing a roaring trade with a fish and chip shop at Guiseley. Ramsden's shop used to catch motorists on their way home from a day in the country and its success led to a huge emporium bearing his name. Before long, Ramsden wanted to move to larger premises, so he sold his shop in Springfield Road, Guiseley, to Jim and Florence Corbett. Consequently the Corbett family left Bradford and moved first to a large terraced house in Oxford Road, Guiseley, and then eventually to a home over their new business.

The house in Oxford Road was a haven for Harry and Leslie, who had the upper floor all to themselves. This enabled them to indulge in their passion for Hornby model railways (they had a large layout) and Meccano. Harry also owned a chemistry set and once experimented with making black boot polish. All was going smoothly until he added the final crucial ingredient and the whole lot bubbled up violently and left a horrible sticky mess over the table. Apart from the usual arguments, as brothers go they got on pretty well. Leslie certainly developed a good relationship with the area — to this day he lives in Oxford Road, opposite the old family home.

The shop in Springfield Road is still thriving. Under its present owners, it was awarded the title "Best Fish and Chip Shop in Great Britain" after being nominated by a listener in a 1982 competition run by disc jockey David Jensen on BBC Radio One.

Fish and chips played an important part in Harry's showbusiness career for, at the age of eleven, he had taken his first tentative steps towards becoming a public entertainer when he played the piano on the opening night of Harry Ramsden's. Harry had been studying the piano since he was seven and had developed into a talented performer. Indeed, he had been Bradford area champion in a national piano competition and his prowess was sufficient to warrant local newspaper coverage. Now in the room directly above his parents' shop, he spent hours playing the works of Bach, Beethoven and Handel while the customers listened appreciatively below and waited for their pennorth of chips.

Harry's parents wanted him to become a concert pianist and to this end bought him the finest piano they could afford, a magnificent Steinway grand which cost £300 then and is worth some £5,000 now. But, in spite of encouragement from his tutor, Herbert Towning of Great Horton, near Bradford, Harry never harboured any real ambition to become a professional pianist. This was partly due to hereditary deafness which affected him from his teenage years. Both his mother and his aunt were deaf and his condition was such that at school he used to have to sit at the front of the class to hear. On leaving school, he got a job with a a large electrical firm in Guiseley, Crompton Parkinson, and his piano lessons steadily drifted. "They started to lapse when we moved to Guiseley," recalled Harry, "because it was simply too much travelling to Great Horton. Herbert wasn't very pleased — he had high hopes for me. I still used to play above the shop, though. My regular partner was Reg Dale, a teacher at Carlton High School, Bradford, where I had been a pupil. We bought a book of Beethoven duets and had some marvellous nights playing the piano, then table tennis for an hour, more piano and rounding the evening off with a fish and chip supper."

Leslie Corbett was a keen saxophonist but his love of jazz didn't compliment Harry's classical approach. However, at the start of the Second World War, together with a drummer appropriately named Eric Guiseley, they formed a trio, The Rythmists, and played over the shop. On closing days, Leslie used to nip downstairs to belt out his jazz numbers because the tiled walls of the shop were acoustically perfect for the saxophone. "We must have had very tolerant neighbours, " he reflects.

When Harry was twenty-four, he suddenly decided to take up music again seriously. "Herbert Towning was very keen for me to sit for my LRAM exam and become a Licentiate of the Royal Academy of Music. I was nearly ready to take it when I received a letter saying that while up a ladder fixing a tile on his roof, Herbert Towning had suffered a heart attack, fallen off the ladder and died. You could have knocked me down with a feather! Once I'd recovered from the shock, I took a few lessons with another teacher for a year but when I told him I was getting married, he predicted that marital status would put an end to my studies. And of course he was right. When you're newly married, you haven't got the time or the inclination for things like piano lessons. So I never did take the exam."

In 1942, Harry had met Marjorie, a lively nineteen-year-old waitress at Harry Ramsden's, and he used to ride round to her house on his 500cc Norton motorcycle. Incidentally, he was also an ardent cyclist and would pedal the length and breadth of the Yorkshire Dales, thinking nothing of riding to the east coast and back in one day. Leslie meanwhile had joined the RAF (Harry's deafness prevented him from serving in the war) and once when he came home on leave, Harry fixed him up on a date with a girl named Muriel who was a secretary at Crompton Parkinson. Two years later, on 8 July, 1944, the foursome had a joint wedding at Guiseley Parish Church.

Little did Harry know it at the time but one of Leslie's wartime homecomings was to be of considerable importance. To celebrate it, Harry suggested that the family should stage a small concert party above their fish and chip shop, and he and Muriel set about writing a melodrama at work. Harry played the arch villain with Muriel as the poor heroine tied to the railroad track. "It was pretty amateurish stuff," admitted Harry, "but good fun nonetheless." However the party did provide him with a new hobby which was to play a significant part in his future — magic.

"A chap at work had taught me a few card tricks so at this party I did those as a character called The

Great Corbett, resplendent in a moustache of soot. Amazingly, they went down really well. It was something I seemed to take to naturally. I thought how interesting it all was and promptly went out and bought some magic books and started practising. I was hooked.

"After a few weeks, I went in to our grocer's and when it was a bit quiet in the shop and there were no customers around, I showed him my card tricks. He seemed quite impressed. I told him I'd even got a half-hour act worked out for parties. 'Leave it to me,' he said and to my amazement within a day or two, he came back and said he'd fixed me up with a kids' party at the local bank manager's. Now it was one thing doing tricks in the grocer's shop but another matter altogether performing in front of a host of children. I was a bag of nerves. Marjorie could see through all my tricks — I could fool other people but I could never fool her. She'd always say: 'I know how you did that.' But being a supportive wife, she deliberately used to look the other way at the crucial moment.

"In spite of my apprehension, the party went well. Everyone seemed happy and at the end the bank manager asked:

"'What about your fee?'

"'I don't want paying,' I replied.

"'But I insist. How are you fixed for playing cards?' he asked, because you couldn't get them at that time. And he gave me six brand new packs. I was knocked out — it was my first fee."

Harry caught the conjuring bug and became a firm favourite at children's parties in the Bradford area. In 1947, he left Crompton Parkinson to work as an engineer's surveyor with the Vulcan Boiler Insurance Company. "I'd always wanted letters after my name and within six months of joining Vulcan, I was able to become an Associate Member of the Institute of Electrical Engineers. So I was Harry Corbett, A.M.I.E.E. Of course if I'd have stuck with my piano lessons, I would have been Harry Corbett, A.M.

I.E.E., L.R.A.M. But anyway having letters after my name was a great step up for me." However it was nothing compared to the consequences of the annual works' holiday of 1948. For it was then that Harry took the family to Blackpool and bought the glove puppet that was to change his life.

"I suppose the teddy bear was really bought to amuse the children," admitted Harry, "but you know what kids are like at that age, they play with something for a bit and then get bored with it. I'd have the puppet peering from around the lapel of my jacket and David would stroke it but I think it only amused him for about ten minutes. Then he was off to play with something else. But I fell in love with it. It was so natural for me as my large hands gave me a big stretch and made it so much easier to manipulate the puppet; on people with smaller hands puppets can look rheumatic. And the dexterity acquired from playing the piano undoubtedly helped too. I was strongly into the magic by then so I had this feeling straight away that the teddy could somehow be used in the act. It was just a question of working out exactly how. At the time, I was having magic lessons from a chap in Leeds, George Blake, who charged me £1 a go. He had a puppet cat for his stage act and at the end of one lesson he said he'd got a little prop he thought might attract me because he knew I'd got a thing about animals.

"'What do you think about this?' he announced, and produced an old felt hat with a hole in the back and sewn into it was exactly the same teddy bear that I'd got at home.

"Astounded, I said: 'I've just bought one of those teddies.'

"He said: 'Well the hat and the teddy are yours for nothing if you want them but you'll have to work out your own routine.'

"So the basic and all-important idea of having the puppet sewn into the hat was really down to

George Blake. He had the know-how but didn't know what to do with it."

Harry did. First he bought what was to become Sooty's trademark, a water-pistol. "It was just something for the teddy to do, give the kiddies a squirt of water and get a laugh. There was nothing more to it than that, it was just a bit of harmless fun." Then he worked out a card routine which, with the puppet sewn into the hat, made it appear that the bear was doing the tricks. At first, it was just a six-minute spot in Harry's hour-long magic act. "Straight away the kids loved it," recalled Harry. "They thought the teddy was so real and they were fascinated by him finding the card. I also did a piece of business where teddy tapped an empty jar with his magic wand and it suddenly appeared full of sweets. Then teddy used to throw the sweets to the children in the audience but it quickly developed into a free-for-all, so I thought it best to cut out the sweet distribution before we had World War Three on our hands. The teddy quickly became the star and I was relegated to the role of his assistant. The kids weren't bothered about me. I began to realise I'd got something here, so I thought I'd better concentrate more and more on the teddy. I built him a little table on which to do his card tricks and he simply took over. It got to the stage where audiences were putting up with my conjuring but were really looking forward to the teddy bear. I knew I had to re-structure the act completely and before long I had worked out a half-hour show with teddy doing it all."

By 1950, Harry was advertising the teddy in local newspapers for children's parties in the Leeds/Bradford area and simultaneously he decided to introduce his creation to an older audience. "I was booked for Pudsey Conservative Club and I told the organiser: 'I've got a full hour of magic, tried and tested, or I've got a brand new half-hour act with a teddy bear. I think he's a knockout but it's up to you. Which do you want? I'll tell you what, if I do my new act and you don't like him, you can have your money back. There'll be no fee.'" There was never any question of Harry not being paid as he and his teddy went down a storm. He was now convinced he was on to a winner.

A friend and neighbour of Harry's in Guiseley was Barney Colehan, a BBC producer who later went on to create those perennial television favourites *The Good Old Days* and *It's a Knockout* as well as working with puppet pigs Pinky and Perky. But at the start of the Fifties he was best-known as the Barney in Wilfred Pickles' catchphrase "Give 'em the money, Barney" from the hugely successful radio series *Have a Go*. Colehan was devising a pilot radio programme from Leeds called *Happy Families* which was to feature particularly talented families. He remembered Harry on piano and brother Leslie on saxophone performing above the fish and chip shop in Guiseley and invited them to appear on the show. There was no magic and no teddy, just music. The Corbetts were joined by Fred and Bert, The Gaunt Brothers, who were pianists, and by The Wallis Family whose leading light, comedian Peter Wallis, is still going strong today. And the compere was Michael Miles who, from 1955, was to throw the nation into a quandary by asking whether a contestant should take the money or open the box in the long-running television game show *Take Your Pick*.

"Happy Families worked well enough, " recalls Colehan "but it was never followed up to become a series. " Anyway, Barney was busy with *Have a Go*. In those days it was just him, Wilfred Pickles and Violet Carson at the piano. It was long before Pickles' wife Mabel had ever been heard of as a celebrity in her own right — she just used to sit in the audience then. Because of *Have a Go's* phenomenal popularity, the Government wanted Pickles to go on a tour of northern coalfields to boost miners' morale and hopefully therefore their production. But the BBC was not in favour of this. They wouldn't allow Barney Colehan to go and Violet Carson (who a decade later turned *Coronation Street*'s hair-netted harridan Ena Sharples into a national figure and royal favourite) also refused to have anything to do with it. Pickles wanted to press ahead with a six-week tour. However, with Violet pulling out, he needed a pianist. Colehan says: "I told Pickles I knew a young fellow named Harry Corbett who did magic and played the piano. I thought the combination would be ideal for entertaining the miners' children. I didn't know anything about his teddy bear."

Harry was determined to make a success of the tour and painstakingly studied Violet's style of piano playing. "Although Barney Colehan was a pal and regularly used to come round to our house for sing-songs at the piano, I was absolutely knocked out that he'd even think about me to take Violet Carson's place. I did have one thing going for me though. Wilfred Pickles rather favoured people with an affliction, he was renowned for it, and he often employed a blind accordionist. My hearing was so bad by then that I had to wear a hearing aid with a large band around my head. So I suppose I fitted in nicely!"

Harry and teddy were a big hit on the tour, which provided Harry with valuable experience in the art of stage work. And it was all because Violet Carson didn't want to go. So not a lot of people know that indirectly Sooty owes a considerable debt to Ena Sharples. . .

On his return, Harry continued to perform locally with his puppet. Already Marjorie Corbett had noticed the remarkable transformation in her husband whenever he put the teddy on. "He was like Jekyll and Hyde," she says. "Harry was basically a very quiet, shy man, but once he'd got that bear on, there was no stopping him — he was always laughing. It brought him right out of his shell. His hesitancy and shyness vanished so that he was completely at ease. He became a natural performer."

But his hearing continued to give cause for concern. His brother Leslie says: "Harry's trouble was that the bones of his inner ear had virtually seized up. Yet the strange thing about his deafness was that when he went into a factory, he seemed to be able to hear a lot better than I could. Amidst all the noise, I could never understand what people were saying unless they shouted, yet Harry was all right. Perhaps the vibration of the machines was keeping his ear free."

In the evenings, Harry used to play the piano at the Royal Hotel, Ilkley, and one night a lady who was a regular visitor there told him about a revolutionary new operation that she had had done. It was called a fenestration and involved a small "window" being inserted behind the ear. She said it had worked wonders for her. It sounded just what Harry needed, so he consulted a Harley Street surgeon. "The surgeon painted the most awful picture," said Harry. "In his opinion there was only a fifty-fifty chance of success, a thirty-five per cent chance that my hearing would be worse and a ten per cent chance of my face being paralysed. It sounded far too dangerous to take a chance on. However on reflection, I think the reason Harley Street didn't want to know was because I hadn't any money.

"Fortunately, this lady knew of another surgeon in Scotland, a Dr. Simpson Hall, who was reputed to be the best in the world. He had no doubts whatsoever; he said he could definitely help me. So I went up to Edinburgh and had this fenestration operation on my left ear. I expected to be able to hear immediately afterwards but to my horror it took months and I arrived home actually feeling worse than when I had gone. All my sense of balance had disappeared and I felt constantly dizzy. Marjorie said when I walked through the door, I was green.

"Luckily, my hearing gradually improved. They used to test it by using a tape measure and a watch and measuring how far away I could hear the ticking of the watch. The first time I knew I was better was when I could hear the note lingering while I was playing the Steinway piano. It was a tremendous feeling. But there was one minor problem — Simpson Hall's bill. When I got home, I worried to hell about how I was going to pay him — after all, I had nothing in the bank. But Simpson Hall was a marvellous dour Scot. He said: 'Don't worry, I won't charge you. Just make a contribution to the nursing home where you stayed.' I think he simply enjoyed the success of performing an operation that was considered by many to be too great a risk."

Now recovered, Harry's fame spread. In March 1951, no less an organ than the *Wharfedale Observer* eulogised: "The sight of a toy teddy bear doing conjuring tricks 'on his own' has proved to have an irresistible appeal for youngsters." Yorkshire folk used to tell Harry he should be on that new-fangled idea, television. Mind you, in 1950 less than one house in twenty actually owned a set. But the idea steadily grew in Harry's mind so he telephoned his pal Barney Colehan. "Harry said the tour with Wilfred Pickles had taught him a lot," says Colehan, "and now he wanted some advice on his magic act.

"I said: 'I've seen your magic act a hundred times, Harry. I know what you do.'

"'But this is completely different,' he said. 'It's something new I've devised.'

"So he came to my office, reached in his case and produced this teddy bear glove puppet. It wasn't very sophisticated, but I was astounded that this thing on Harry's hand was able to play the xylophone and appear to be doing tricks! He did the full routine, including the water-pistol and the hammer, and because Harry was good enough to have been a classical pianist, the xylophone presented no problem. He asked me if there was any chance of him doing a little show on television and I said: 'As a matter of fact there's a *Talent Night* at the Radio and Television Industries' Exhibition at the City Hall, Manchester, this week.'

"Derek Burrell-Davis, a BBC producer from the North, was in charge of the auditions and I told him about Harry's act. He said he'd seen so many puppets, he'd had them up to here. He did not want to see another puppet act. I said: 'I wouldn't waste your time if it wasn't any good but this one's different. It does remarkable magic tricks and plays the xylophone.'"

Burrell-Davis relented and Harry was told to go to Manchester that Friday for what was nothing more than a closed-circuit show, seen by members of the industry. Harry did his routine just as Eric Fawcett, the producer of the gala show that was being networked live to the entire country the following night, arrived from London. Harry said: "He walked in, saw my act and immediately said: 'I want that in tomorrow's show. But cut it down to four and a half minutes because the programme's already set.' I was floored — I was going to be seen all over the country at peak viewing time. I just couldn't believe this was really happening, it was like a fairy tale. I hadn't even thought seriously about television until I'd seen Barney Colehan on the Wednesday, and on the Saturday I was going to be on screen. I stayed awake virtually all that night trying to shorten the act. By three in the morning I'd still only got it down to six minutes, so I decided I'd better get some sleep. When I saw Eric Fawcett the next day, I showed him this routine of teddy with a live hamster but explained that it was still six minutes long. He said it was perfect and that I was not to alter a thing, adding: 'Don't tell the other acts but I'll squeeze them for time.'"

And so Harry Corbett and his teddy made their television debut in *Talent Night* on Saturday 3, May 1952. The comedian Jimmy James was the compere and the show was introduced by the debonair McDonald Hobley who, along with the likes of Sylvia Peters and Mary Malcolm, was one of the BBC's leading personalities of the day. "Obviously I was nervous but once I glanced to one side and saw Mac Hobley beaming all over his face, I was away," said Harry, just as excited at the recollection thirty-seven years on. "We went down an absolute bomb — there was no doubt about it, we were the hit of the show. Afterwards, everyone from the producer down rushed up to congratulate me and said: 'We'll see you on BBC in the autumn. It's bound to happen.'"

The newspapers gave the pair rave reviews. The *Sunday Express* of 4 May enthused: "Five minutes on the television screen last night established Harry Corbett's teddy bear as a rival to Muffin the Mule." The *News Chronicle* added: "Mr. Corbett should certainly introduce his puppet to children's television."

Eric Fawcett was equally thrilled. He phoned Harry on the Sunday morning and said: "I was thinking in bed last night about you and your teddy bear. You'll definitely go far, you're absolutely made to measure for television, but you've got to make your puppet different from other toy bears. Everyone has a teddy bear looking like that. You must alter its appearance and give it a distinctive expression to make it yours. Above all, give it a name. And don't forget to register the name for copyright and have photographs taken of it from all angles, including the back. It's a lot of effort but believe me it will be worth it."

So what could Harry and Marjorie do to a teddy bear to make it look more commercial? They tried making it all black but that didn't work at all and then they hit on the idea of just blacking his ears and nose with some soot from the chimney. That was much better. Now for a name. Well, he's smothered in soot — so how about Sooty? They both agreed on it immediately. It had just the right hint of mucky mischief that was appropriate to a little boy character and it was short enough for children to remember. The name was duly registered and Harry and Sooty were ready to take the nation by storm. But some agonising decisions lay ahead.

CHAPTER TWO

IZZY WHIZZY, LET'S GET BUSY

The BBC kept its word. Freda Lingstrom, the formidable Head of Children's Programmes, asked Harry and Sooty to appear in *Saturday Special*, a new series starring comedian Peter Butterworth which was to be made in October. It would be screened every two weeks, alternating with *Whirligig*, a great children's favourite of the time which boasted such characters as Hank the cowboy, Mexican Pete the bandit, who delighted in singing the Mexican Hat Dance, and Big Chief Dirty Face. Then there was the unsavoury Mr. Turnip who was the bane of Humphrey Lestocq, known for his catchphrase "Goody goody gumdrops." *Whirligig* was a major stepping-stone for many careers. For example it launched a young Australian entertainer named Rolf Harris, who used to appear with Willoughby, a drawing board with a life of its own. Saturday Special was seen as an equally important showcase for new talent and Freda Lingstrom was particularly fascinated as to how Harry had come to create Sooty.

"Did you get the idea from Annette Mills and her puppet Prudence Kitten?" she asked.

"Certainly not," replied Harry, mildly offended at the suggestion. "I've never ever seen Prudence Kitten. I couldn't — we haven't got a television set."

Lingstrom wanted Sooty as the ship's

mascot on the *S. S. Saturday Special*, but she warned Harry not to give up his day job just yet. After all, like most things in television in the early Fifties, the programme was an unknown factor — it might not last beyond the initial run of six shows.

Money was the key factor. Harry had been paid £10 for *Talent Night* plus a third-class return rail fare between Leeds and Manchester (13s 0d) and one night's subsistence allowance of 32s 6d. For *Saturday Special*, he would receive twelve guineas a show but since the programmes were only fortnightly, if he did decide to turn professional, he would have to support his family on just six guineas a week for twelve weeks. At the time, he was getting around £15 a week as an electrical engineer with Vulcan in addition to his fees from his part-time conjuring.

It was a difficult decision. Harry desperately wanted to prove himself as a full-time entertainer and he knew from the enthusiasm that greeted Sooty's every appearance that his golden bear could eventually turn into a gold mine. But could he put his family at risk by going professional at this stage? He and Marjorie talked about it long and hard. In the end, just as it had been she who had convinced him that he should buy Sooty in the first place, it was Marjorie who again made up Harry's mind for him. She told him fair and square: "Throw up your job. I don't want my old age ruined by you saying 'I wonder what would have happened if I'd done television when I had the chance.' The only thing to do is do it. If it doesn't work, you can always find yourself another job — you're young enough and you've got the qualifications."

So at the age of thirty-four, Harry decided he would give it a go. But before he took the plunge on a full-time basis, he wrote to Vulcan asking for permission to take six Saturdays off in October. "I said it was for live television shows in London and that they should take the time off from my holidays. They were most indignant. They wrote back and said: 'No, you can't have permission.

You can't do television AND engineering — it's your choice. We've got two hundred engineers all over the country, a lot of whom have television sets. If they see you, they'll say: "what's he doing on television? In that case we'll do a bit of sidelining and start something up ourselves." You can't do it. It's got to be one or the other.' So I handed in my notice there and then.

"However I soon realised we couldn't live on six guineas a week, so I thought about getting a job as a TV salesman. I thought if I go to sell someone a television set and I'm on the screen, I'm halfway in. I've got one foot in the door. I decided to write to Pye and Marconi and actually had an interview with Pye coming up. But I never got round to it. Things moved much too fast with Sooty."

Since the Corbetts couldn't afford a TV set (at the time fewer than two million Britons owned one), Marjorie had to take the boys on a three-mile bus ride from their home in Guiseley to a friend's house to watch their father on *Saturday Special*. Young Peter (now better known to millions as Matthew Corbett) was four at the time. He says: "It was my first real recollection of Sooty, although I'm told that when my father came on screen I didn't even recognise him. He appeared with a sweeping brush and apparently I asked: 'Who's that?'"

Saturday Special was a great success but it didn't pay the bills. Marjorie was beginning to have second thoughts about the whole business. "I hadn't realised that the registering and copyrighting of Sooty would cost so much. Harry was forever sending off seven guineas for this and ten guineas for that. But we had no money. I remember going to Harry a few weeks after he'd started and saying: 'Look lovey, this is all right but when is the money going to start coming IN? I've got two children to clothe and feed.'

"It was a big responsibility for me," says Marjorie looking back on those times of financial constraint. "If you had two children in those days you got five shillings a week from the government. I remember once I needed to buy something in the food line and I had no money so I went to the Post Office. I had four weeks' money owing but I didn't want to draw it all out in one go. I asked the woman behind the counter:

"'Could I just cash the first one please?'

"She really showed me up, answering in a loud voice so all the other customers could hear: 'Mrs. Corbett, you cannot just have one week. You draw it all or you have nothing. '

"'I'll have it all then,' I replied sheepishly."

But Harry knew things would get better and that the money would start coming in. He and his charge soon graduated to a series of programmes entitled *Sooty the Teddy Bear Magician*. Harry wrote the familiar theme music in an hour and each show ended with Sooty rattling out The "Teddy Bear's Picnic" on the xylophone before waving "bye-bye." After the very first show, Harry was contacted by a man from Barnsley who wanted the rights to make Sooty's xylophones. Harry didn't hesitate about accepting and signed a one-year deal. This was where all the effort of copyrighting started to pay off. Next to approach him was the Chad Valley Toy Company who wanted to make the Sooty puppets. "This was the one I'd been waiting for — the opportunity to get the puppets on the market. One of the things that had influenced me about going full-time was that I had read about a firm called Muffin Syndicate Limited who handled all the royalties for Muffin the Mule with Annette Mills, sister of John Mills the actor. They had a turnover of £30,000 a year. I thought if I can get anywhere near that, I'll be delighted." So Sooty Limited was founded, the registered office being Harry and Marjorie's semi in Guiseley. This twelve-inch puppet was becoming big business.

Much of the success in any business is down to timing, and there's no doubt that Harry Corbett and Sooty came along at exactly the right time. At the start of the Fifties, television was nothing more than a novelty

— and an expensive one at that since a new set cost around £85. That figure doesn't sound much now but to put it in perspective, you could buy a smart three-bedroomed semi for £2,000 and a new car for £400. But the screening of the Coronation in 1953 gave a massive boost to the sales of sets, both before and after the event. Radio was forced to take a back seat and inevitably as television became more important, so did its stars. Before long virtually every house in the country had a television aerial which meant that the viewing nation was brought up with Harry and Sooty. Everybody knew them. Also Sooty's only serious rival in the hearts of Fifties' children was Muffin the Mule. Not only was clanky old Muffin about as cuddly as Meccano, but the competition soon ended anyway when Annette Mills, who had never enjoyed the best of health, died in 1955 at the age of sixty-one. True, characters like Billy Bean, Bengo, Andy Pandy, The Flowerpot Men, Rag, Tag and Bobtail, The Woodentops and Annette Mills' other creation Prudence Kitten were all children's favourites, but none were marketed with the same vigour as Sooty.

Neither were they as appealing. No self-respecting child could get attached to someone with Andy Pandy's dress sense, Rag, Tag and Bobtail were little more than vermin while taking The Woodentops to bed would more likely give you splinters than a good night's sleep. The other great advantage of Sooty was that being a glove puppet, anybody could work him. There was no need for a yard and a half of strings.

Sooty's personality was designed to prove irresistible to youngsters. Harry Corbett described him as "a lovable, but naughty, little boy teddy bear of five years old who gets away with the sort of things all children would like to. As with Peter Pan, he never gets any older." And there is a very simple reason why it never occurred to the Corbetts to make Sooty speak. For at first it was just a one-man show and that man, Harry, was no ventriloquist. So there was no way that Sooty would have been able to say anything. Sooty's physical appearance was equally well defined. The old sharp-featured bear that Marjorie said resembled a rat had by now been replaced by a much cuter, cuddlier version. The whereabouts of that original teddy is a greater mystery than the Marie Celeste. Many people claim to have very early Sootys (disc jockey Mike Read, a confirmed Sooty fan, bought one at an auction not long ago) but nobody, least of all Harry, seems to know what happened to the founder of the Sooty dynasty.

Although of course we all know that like Santa Claus, there is only one Sooty, he has to have plenty of helpers for those moments when even the most biological of washing powders can't remove awkward unmentionable stains. Harry was very particular about Sooty's look and was determined that Chad Valley should get it right, particularly the eyes and ears. "I must have driven them mad. I remember once getting six Sootys from them and I sent them all back with a label attached to each one's ear, saying what was wrong. Even with a good batch, I'd often ask Marjorie to add a few stitches to some of the noses so they looked absolutely right.

"Chad Valley told me: 'We think it's impossible to please you, Mr. Corbett. You're never happy with the puppets.'

"'Oh yes I am,' I said, 'when I get the right one. But a lot of them simply aren't right.'

"I decided the only thing for it was to go to the Chad Valley factory at Wellington, Shropshire, and sort it out myself. I spent three days there at the side of the woman who made them, telling her exactly what I did and didn't like about the puppets. In the end, I came away with seventy-two Sootys. It was so important because they didn't last very long. I thought that batch of seventy-two would last me forever but in less than two years they were all gone because every time one gets messed up and covered in jam or treacle, that's it. It doesn't wash out."

Leslie Corbett remembers how Harry used

to "break in" a new puppet. "He carried around a knitting needle to loosen the woollen stuffing in the head of a new Sooty so that he could operate it properly with his fingers. He'd stick this great needle up the inside of the puppet and pull the stuffing around inside the head. Knowing Harry, I'm sure he felt very guilty about re-arranging Sooty's brains with a needle!"

Harry's own character was also to become an integral part of the act. Children loved to see his face covered in ink or flour, the victim of yet another of Sooty's pranks, while parents everywhere sympathised with that harassed, brow-beaten look as he uttered those familiar closing words: "Bye bye everybody. Bye bye." Not everyone saw the funny side though. Once Sooty thought he would bake a cake on the show and put the ingredients of flour and eggs in a basket. He shook his head, waved his wand and the whole basket rose into the air on a wire and began to tilt precariously. As the camera cut back, a studio hand out of shot ripped open a one pound bag of flour and tipped the contents over Harry. This was followed by two eggs, thrown down on to the top of his head so that they smashed and oozed down his face. Never had Harry been in such a mess. "I always used to wear a good suit because if you wore overalls, the kids would know right at the start that something messy was going to happen and it wouldn't be as funny. This one was in a right state but I peeled it off and took it along as usual to the BBC wardrobe department who always cleaned my suits. But when I returned to collect it two weeks later, it was still bundled up in a corner where I'd left it. Attached to it was a curt note which read: 'In future please take your suits back home and clean them yourself.'

"After that I started taking them to a cleaner in Bradford. Every week, I'd turn up with a suit plastered with raw egg and flour. The manager thought I was a raving lunatic!"

The year of 1953 had begun well for Harry

and Sooty. Their television work included a series called *Sooty Introduces* where the little bear presented acts new to television. Not surprisingly, Harry couldn't remember any stars of the future among them, for it is doubtful whether anyone's career would be greatly enhanced by being introduced by a silent compere. But Harry's fame was spreading and he was offered a seventeen-week summer season with Butlin's at their three big camps — Filey, Skegness and Clacton. With the prospect of more money coming in, the Corbetts splashed out on a TV set. "With Harry appearing regularly, we thought it was about time we bought one," recalls Marjorie. And after the success of the fenestration operation on his left ear, Harry decided to pay a return visit to Dr. Simpson Hall to have similar surgery performed on the right one. "This time, because I was earning a bit from TV, I thought I could definitely pay him," said Harry. "Again at the end, he said no fee. I was determined to repay him in some way so I thought about buying him something. I knew he liked hunting, shooting and fishing so I asked his secretary whether he would appreciate a new gun. She said he'd got absolutely everything. So I had to settle for giving another donation to the nursing home. I was so grateful to the man — I don't think I could have been on television without the operations. Then again, had I not been deaf, life would also have been totally different. My ambition had been to go into sales work with the engineering firm and it was only my deafness that put a stop to that. If I had been able to pursue that career, I would never have got into doing those part-time shows."

While negotiating the deal with Butlin's, the holiday camp executives expressed surprise that Harry hadn't yet got himself an agent and recommended a lady named Pearl Beresford. "She was a hard woman," said Harry, "I think she grew hair on her teeth! But she was invaluable to me as I was a bit naive when it came to financial matters." One of the first things she did was to sort out the Chad Valley contract. "I'd signed up all the commercial rights to Chad Valley and Pearl said: 'You shouldn't have done that, Harry, you could have got a better deal.' She spotted that the contract was coming up for renewal and told me to keep quiet, not to ring or write to them, as they had to give me a month's notice if they wanted to carry on for another year. She let the contract expire and then left it for a couple of weeks.

"'Right,' she said. 'We've got them.' She asked Chad Valley if they wanted to renew the contract.

"'Of course we do,' they replied, somewhat taken aback.

"'In which case, it will be a completely new one,' she announced. 'You can have the rights to make the Sooty puppets only — you don't do anything else without first consulting us.' To put it mildly, they were shocked. But of course she was quite right."

Meanwhile the Butlin's tour had been a mixed blessing; while providing further experience and exposure, it also laid the foundations of twenty years of illness for Harry. "My work schedule was a killer. From home in Guiseley, I'd travel to Filey where I did two shows on the Monday; on the Tuesday, I put on two shows for a friend in Scarborough; on Wednesday, it was Butlin's Skegness; on Thursday, I drove down to Clacton; and to make matters worse, that summer we did *Sooty Introduces,* so I had to be in London on Friday before travelling back to Guiseley and starting all over again. And I did that for seventeen weeks. Marj hardly saw me. By the eighth week of the tour I was in a fish and chip shop in Skegness and all the rushing around without any help, driving a thousand miles a week in a Morris Minor, missing meals and drinking stale ale had filled me up with pain. So I called the doctor. He said: 'You've got a duodenal ulcer. Have you got a job with a lot of dashing about and a lot of worry and stress?' That summed it up perfectly. 'Anyway,' he said, 'you'll be in dire trouble unless you change.' After that diagnosis, I eased the load a bit for the remainder of the tour by employing a lad from college to be my driver. But that summer was the start of my ulcer."

Marjorie says: "He used to frighten me with that ulcer. There were times when I'd come in to find him writhing around on the floor in agony with it. The worse thing was there was nothing I could do about it — I felt so helpless. Eating was such a problem for him, everything had to be plain, no rich sauces. Many's the time we'd just be looking at the menu in a restaurant and he'd have to ask for a slice of bread and butter. He had to have something to chew to stop the churning in his stomach. And Harry had all that for twenty years. But the show always went on."

During the Butlin's tour, Harry was given an early indication of the appeal Sooty held for adults as well as children. Harry recalled: "After my diagnosis, Sir Billy Butlin himself came to see me with some champagne and the camp doctor. I remember that for some reason Sir Billy sat in the wash basin in the corner of the chalet. Anyway, the doctor looked at my case and asked whether I'd got Sooty in there and would I lift him out. Naturally I obliged and introduced him to Sooty. To my amazement, he soon became oblivious to everyone else in the room except Sooty. This doctor started talking at great length about real medical cases and was actually giving Sooty a serious lecture on medicine. All Sooty was doing was listening. Anyway, the doctor was wasting his time because I don't think Sooty understood any of the Latin names. . . "

One of Harry's favourite routines with Butlin's was one where Sooty caught three or four cardboard fish before finally landing a real goldfish. "The goldfish used to travel everywhere with me," said Harry. "I kept it in a bowl, covered with a wash leather held in place with an elastic band; I used to put the bowl in the boot of the Morris Minor. But it was a real nuisance having to cart this damn fish to Filey, Skegness and Clacton every week. Eventually, it dawned on me how crazy this was and how much simpler it would be instead if I bought three bowls and three fish and left one at each camp. So that's what I did and I arranged to leave the bowl with the respective Tannoy offices where they made all the camp announcements.

"I arrived at Clacton one week and went to the office to collect the goldfish bowl as usual, only to be greeted by long faces.

"'Sorry,' they said. 'It's dead.'

"'How? What happened?'

"'Well,' they explained awkwardly, 'it was so hot in the office that we put the fish into a bigger bowl and moved it into the foyer so that it could get more air. But unfortunately, everybody walking through the foyer used it as an ashtray!'

"I went along to the foyer and there was this fish floating lifeless in a sea of cigarette ash. The water was so thick you could hardly see the poor creature. We had to rush around to a pet shop to buy a replacement before the show."

Harry nearly lost another goldfish while changing its water at home. "I put it in some water in the wash-basin and suddenly, to my horror, I noticed steam rising. I'd only switched the hot tap on by mistake. Talk about fried fish! Needless to say, it looked a hopeless cause — the fish was floating upside down. So I went downstairs to put it in the dust-bin. Young Peter, who was about six at the time, spotted me.

"'Isn't that my fish?' he asked, because we'd let him adopt one.

"'Yes, but I'm afraid it's dead,' I answered.

"'No, it's not. I saw it twitch.'

"I said: 'Well it nearly is. I'm going to put it in the bin.'

"'You can't do that. Put it in some water and it will be all right in the morning.'

"Reluctantly I agreed, but the next day it

was still perpendicular. I'd seen more life in fish coated with breadcrumbs.

"'Just give it another day,' Peter insisted.

"I did as he asked and went in expecting to find a corpse, but the fish was swimming around merrily as if nothing had happened. It must have spent the two days in a profound state of shock. And so, miraculously, it was able to resume its showbusiness career."

By now Sooty was being bombarded with presents from his young fans and was receiving in the region of four hundred letters a month. Unlike other stars, his mail was more likely to contain jelly babies and dolly mixtures than proposals of marriage. The BBC recognised his pulling power too, and soon rewarded Harry with a two-year contract (quite an achievement in those days) to do a weekly series of *The Sooty Show*. "From about 1955 onwards were the golden years," enthused Harry. "There was simply no competition. "

One of the great features of *The Sooty Show* were the marvellous miniature props, all made years before the Japanese had thought of micro-industry. These were far more than just little toys, they were superb examples of precision engineering, all of which were fully operational. Among the most ingenious was the mincer which fed out complete sausages, a pottery wheel in which the worm and pinion gears had to be cut specially so that they remained silent during a live transmission and the trick camera that, no matter in which direction it was pointed, always squirted ink over the hapless Harry.

They were all the work of Bill Garrett, who had worked at the same firm as Harry, Crompton Parkinson, for twenty-eight years. Raised in the National Children's Home, Bill had joined Crompton Parkinson on leaving school and in his spare time, he used to make items of furniture. Harry was a skilled craftsman himself, but with Sooty's world rapidly expanding, he soon realised he needed help with making the props for the show. "So I asked Bill to become my full-time prop maker. He said: 'I'll have to think hard about that, Harry' but a couple of days later he came back to me and said he'd give it a go. 'But I shall have to ask £18 a week,' he added apprehensively. I could just about afford that and anyway I reckoned Bill was a sound investment, so he joined me. Mind you, I was taking a chance. When I took him on, a friend of Bill's said that Bill had had such an awful life (besides his lonely childhood, he'd had an unhappy first marriage) that he'd murder anyone who let him down. That was the last thing I wanted to do. I said: 'I can assure you I'll do my best for Bill. I have every intention in the world of being successful — but in this business, you never know.'"

Employing Bill Garrett was a major step forward for Harry because his expertise meant the show's horizons could be broadened to include better and better sets. From its humble origins, *The Sooty Show* was now a miniature masterpiece. "Bill didn't just create props," reflected Harry with genuine admiration, "he made collectors' items. They were works of art. He made every instrument in the orchestra, each a perfect working replica of the real thing and each with its own case. Every idea I came up with, he could make. He could make anything in any material. We were driving along once and we pulled up alongside a Rolls-Royce.

"'How much is there in that, Harry?' asked Bill in his matter-of-fact way.

"'Oh, about £15,000,' I replied.

"'I bet I could make one cheaper than that!'

"And I bet he could have too. The man was a genius.

"I remember the first thing he ever constructed was Sooty's fish and chip shop — it seemed a natural choice for me with the family background. He built a marvellous dry cleaning works early on too, a revolving electric organ, a robot called 'Enery that took him five months in all and was valued at £450 and also a special xylophone where whatever tune Sooty played, the corresponding animal popped out. For "Three Blind Mice", there'd be real mice, for "Run Rabbit Run", a flap would open and there'd be a little rabbit and for "How Much Is That Doggie In The Window?" Blossom, our lovely papillon dog, would appear. She was a real favourite on the show.

"Bill was a true perfectionist. I asked him to make a miniature caravan once that was to be seen on screen from the outside only. So it needed little more than the shell. But Bill insisted on furnishing the interior too, complete with a fitted wardrobe and a pump in the kitchen which actually drew water. He was incapable of making anything second-class. He used to work in the basement of his home and his second wife hardly ever saw him. He rarely came up for meals on time and would think nothing of working through the night. Rumour has it that when he had left Crompton Parkinson, it had taken five men to fill his job."

One of Harry's more bizarre requests was for a house that had to collapse when the door was slammed. Bill solved the problem by individually making no fewer than three hundred and forty bricks and drilling holes in each one so that they could be threaded on wires. When the wires were withdrawn, the house would collapse. It was an enormous amount of time and trouble for something that Harry might only ever use once.

Bill totally immersed himself in his work, which could be a hazard in the days of live television. Harry recalled: "On one show, he was so worried that the rocket he'd built hadn't ignited properly that he wandered into shot, totally oblivious to the fact we were on air. The producer shouted: 'Who's that? Bill Garrett? What the hell's he doing in the picture? Get him out of it!' Another time, Bill was concerned about why the special TV set he'd made hadn't exploded on cue. Out of the corner of my eye,

I could see him in a world of his own, examining the set, sorting out the wiring, while I was trying to do a show to five million viewers. I had to waffle to cover up for what was going on beside me. I felt like introducing him to the viewers. You see, he was never bothered about the programme, just as long as his props worked efficiently."

Harry was faced with an even more awkward moment when Bill's electric organ broke down half-way through a live show. "It suddenly stopped without any warning," said Harry. "I thought 'how can I get out of this?' So I turned to the camera and said: 'I'd often wondered what would happen if I was on live television and something went wrong and there was nothing I could do about it. Well, it's happened, Sooty's organ's packed up. We can't use it. That's it.' So I said to Sooty: 'What are we going to do now? . . . Whistle? I can't whistle.' But I did and somehow we filled in for the few remaining minutes. The strange thing in a situation like that is that when it's not your fault, you feel completely relaxed.

"But I remember one show when I certainly wasn't relaxed. It was undoubtedly my worst experience on screen. In fact it made me seriously consider packing in television altogether. We had this scene where Sooty held a bottle of HP Sauce in his paw. When I put the bottle on a table in rehearsals, the producer said: 'Harry, the sound department complained that when you put the bottle down, it sounded like a cannon to them. Can you please be careful?' When we did the show itself, I remembered what he had said and put the sauce bottle down very gently. But I had been concentrating so hard on doing it correctly that I couldn't remember what came next. I froze. My mind went blank. I should have been more professional — I shouldn't have allowed a little thing like that to throw me. But it had. I said to Sooty: 'What do we do next?' Needless to say, he didn't answer. Then I spotted something which triggered my memory and I was away again. When I came off I said: 'That's it, I'm finished with television. I'll never ever go through that again.' In the course of the week, people came up to me and said: 'Very good show on Sunday, Harry.' I said: 'Didn't you notice anything wrong when I put the sauce bottle down?' Nobody had noticed a thing. In reality, it had only lasted a couple of seconds but it had seemed like hours to me. You see, I'm a stickler for getting things exactly right. Nothing less will do."

Early in 1955, the little bear had another opportunity to impress grown-ups after adult fans had requested he be moved to a later time. Besides his usual Sunday afternoon ten-minute slot for children at around 4. 50 pm, he appeared in two half-hour shows at 8pm on a Saturday night under the title *Sooty Entertains*. The producer was Harry's friend Barney Colehan, the man who had been so instrumental in bringing Sooty to the screen in the first place. For his first show in February, Sooty's guests included long-forgotten tap dancers Flack and Lucas and Janet Brown, wife of his old sparring partner from *Saturday Special*, Peter Butterworth. Whereas Peter had often been surprised by the odd rap over the head from Sooty's hammer, an even worse fate befell Janet. "Sooty was giving Janet Brown a bunch of flowers to thank her for being on the programme," said Harry. "So, sounding hurt, I said to him: 'You never give me one.' We had this bunch specially made with a squirter in it, which was full of black water paint which looked like ink. Sooty gave me a dose right in the face but unfortunately it rebounded and splashed all over Janet. Not only was she wearing a light coloured gown, which she had bought for £100 specially for the show, but it was just before she was due to sing her solo number! So poor Janet had to come on and sing in a paint-spattered dress." Remarkably, she remained a close friend of the Corbetts, though I don't know whether she's ever forgiven Sooty.

For that programme Harry was paid £30, but such was Sooty's progress that by the time the second show was made, just three months later, he commanded

£63. His special guests on that occasion were zither queen Shirley Abicair, who only got £37, and the aptly-named Windy Blow, one of the first people ever to want to try and make animals out of balloons. The shows were well received and pulled in the highest ratings for that time of night for twenty weeks. But Harry decided not to do any more as he considered adults to be too fickle. He knew that children were Sooty's most faithful fans.

Hot on the heels of the Janet Brown episode, Sooty inflicted his particular brand of mayhem on more regal company at that year's British Industries Fair at London's Olympia. "We were on the Chad Valley stand, " remembered Harry fondly,"and Sooty and I were introduced to the Queen. She shook hands with Sooty's paw and was surprised to find that he was orange and not white as he appeared on her black and white set. In those days, even royalty could only get black and white.

"Then she asked: 'Has he been behaving himself today?'

"I said: 'Yes, he's been very good, knowing you were coming along Ma'am.'

"'Oh,' she said, 'he hasn't bonked you on the head with his hammer this morning. . . ?'

"I knew that the Queen watched Sooty avidly, because it was said that we were Princess Anne's favourite programme and that she often used to watch it in her nursery. Naturally, I had the water-pistol handy and I was trying to pluck up courage to squirt the Queen, but she was wearing velvet so I thought perhaps I'd better not. Instead I swung round and let Prince Philip have it — straight in the face! The Queen really howled with laughter and Philip laughed too. The press reporters heard the commotion, rushed up and asked what the joke was.

"I calmly replied: 'Oh, Sooty's just squirted the Duke.'

"'Squirted the Duke!' they chorused and they all made a dash for the phones. It was big news the next day. The *Daily Mirror* reported it under the headline: 'Sooty Was So Naughty.' It was a prize moment."

Sooty was also in trouble with the Ilford Home Safety Committee, who complained that Sooty being shown climbing an unsafe ladder on television set a bad example to children. "Sometimes we got away with murder," says Marjorie. "I remember we had Sooty climbing into the back of a TV set which then exploded — they'd never let you show that now."

They didn't always get away with it, however. Once when Sooty hit Harry over the head with his hammer, a six-year-old girl ran on to the stage shouting: "You naughty little bear. How dare you!" The balsa wood hammer was one of Harry's favourite props, although he conceded that being hit with it so often didn't help his bent nose.

In those days, the pianist on *The Sooty Show* was Steve Race, now a veteran of series like *My Music*. He remembers once staying in the next hotel room to Harry Corbett. "Suddenly I heard gales of laughter from the next room, which was particularly odd because I knew Harry was on his own. It turned out to be the very first time Harry had thought of hitting himself over the head with a hammer!"

"The hammer went down very well," said Harry as if remembering a long-lost toy. "The kids loved it. But Freda Lingstrom didn't. 'I don't like you using a hammer, Harry,' she said. 'It sets a very bad example to the children.' Then one day there was a true case about a chap who was reading his Sunday paper when his son whacked him over the head with a real hammer — so hard that he had to go to hospital to have stitches put in the wound.

"The boy's mum said: 'Why did you do that to daddy?'

"'Well Sooty did it,' he replied.

"That was the last straw for Freda. 'Right,'

she stormed. 'That's it. The hammer goes.'"

Occasionally, Harry himself genuinely suffered at the paws of Sooty. Once on TV, he made Sooty throw sawdust in his face but he had his mouth open at the time and swallowed some. "When I got home, I was still coughing and choking.

"'What happened?' said Marjorie.

"'It was Sooty,' I said. 'He threw sawdust right down my throat.'

"'You silly fool, you did it yourself.'

"'Yes, I know that,' I pleaded, 'but all the same he shouldn't have done it!'"

One man whose career owed a lot to Sooty was compact comedian Charlie Drake, who made his West End debut as supporting artist with Harry and company at the Adelphi Theatre in 1955. "Harry gave me my big break," says Charlie. "I remember Harry did the afternoon show and Al Read and Shirley Bassey were on in the evenings. Harry was a sell-out, there wasn't a seat to be had and Al Read was so impressed he told me: 'Charlie, I'll have to find myself a little bear.' I said: 'You won't Al, because that bear's unique. There's not another like Sooty.'" Shirley Bassey was just starting out in showbusiness at the time and she and Harry often used to pop over to a nearby coffee house where during their conversations she confessed that her great ambition in life was to own a white sports car. She can probably just about afford one now.

The advent of ITV in 1955 meant there was a whole new world open to television stars — commercials. Animals had particular appeal to Fifties' audiences, early adverts featuring such diverse creatures as the Brooke Bond chimps (where the first voice-over was by Peter Sellers), the Babycham bambi and the Guinness sea lion. "In those days there was nothing like BBC Enterprises," said Harry. "There was nobody at the BBC we had to consult and who would take a percentage. So with regard to merchandising, we did what we wanted. When Wall's Ice Cream approached us and offered £10,000 for Sooty to do a series of commercials, I was delighted. After all, it was the perfect product for us to endorse. What better combination could there be than Sooty, who's really a little boy, and ice cream? But then Oxo stepped in and offered £2,000 more.

"Pearl Beresford said: 'We've got to do Oxo, Harry.'

"I disagreed. 'We can't. We've had all those meeting with Wall's — they've even made a pilot film.'

"'But there's nothing in writing,' insisted Pearl.

"Wall's were frantic. Their marketing people said they would be discussing an increased offer at a meeting with their directors.

"Pearl laid down the law. "'I'm not waiting for any meeting. You'll make your mind up NOW'

"They thought she was bluffing but she wasn't and when they did finally come back with more money, she said it was too late, that we had accepted another offer.

"'What! You can't do this,' they complained.

"She said, 'I've done it. And it's Oxo.'

"So we made a series of one-minute films for Oxo. With more money coming in, Marjorie and I decided to go on our first Mediterranean cruise. When we stopped off at Naples, we heard that Sooty's Oxo commercial had won first prize at the Monte Carlo International Advertising Festival, beating fifty-nine other entrants. It was the equivalent of winning an Oscar for best commercial. It was a wonderful feeling. We really were on top of the world."

After the years of struggle, Harry and Marjorie certainly deserved their cruise in the Med. And thanks to Sooty, they could afford it. In 1956, the business grossed in the region of £50,000, much of this from merchandising. Until then, most merchandising had been based on films or comic characters, but when Peter Barker Ltd took over the Sooty account from Chad Valley, Barker quickly put his experience with marketing Dan Dare from *The Eagle* comic to good effect. Sooty went on where Muffin the Mule had left off and broke new ground for television characters. A Sooty strip cartoon appeared in the *Daily Mirror*, hand puppets were selling for 10s 6d, Sooty's First Annual was on sale at five shillings (I was a proud owner of such a tome) and there were all manner of other items available from Sooty Concessions Limited, including sweets, xylophones, jigsaws, pyjamas, slippers, wallpaper even toothbrush holders. In total, over forty firms were making the merchandise. Harry's personal empire was growing too. He had two offices, one in London, the other at home in Guiseley, where an additional wing had to be built on to the house for business purposes. He also retained a commercial agent, a personal agent, two secretaries, an artist, two scriptwriters and a props manager. In total, Harry owned one thousand five hundred props. And he trotted out public appearances at £50 a time. He even took the precaution of paying £150 a year to insure for £20,000 the thumb and first two fingers of his right hand, acknowledging that those limbs were his fortune. In that respect, he was the original Goldfinger.

In recognition of their celebrity status, Harry and Sooty were invited to appear in an all-star line-up to celebrate the tenth anniversary of the return of television after the War. Also on the bill were Arthur Askey, Shirley Abicair, Isobel Barnett, Petula Clark, Alma Cogan, David Nixon, Gilbert Harding and those leggy lovelies The Television Toppers. To cap it all, Sooty's 1956 Christmas Appeal raised £13,253 for Children in Need. No wonder one newspaper wrote: "To the phenomena of Britain like the Forth Bridge, Nelson's Column and Sabrina must now be added Harry Corbett and Sooty."

Harry's lifestyle had certainly improved. He now drove a second-hand Bentley and had grown accustomed to staying at the best hotels. "When I first went to London for *Saturday Special* I couldn't afford to stay overnight so I used to catch the milk train back and a pal would pick me up at Leeds at three in the morning. I graduated to a bed and breakfast near Euston at 16s 6d per night and, as I grew more successful, I started staying at the Cumberland Hotel, Marble Arch."

Another favourite haunt was London's Grosvenor House Hotel. Marjorie reminisces about one particular holiday which they broke by staying at the Grosvenor for the night. "Inevitably, Harry had Sooty in his case but he had decided that he wasn't going to take him on the two-week cruise, he was going to leave him at the hotel. Sooty was laid out reverently on a piece of cloth in the case — always face up, we never laid him face down — and Harry gave him to the luggage man. He said: 'Will you put this at the back, I won't be needing it for two weeks, I'll collect it on the way home.' We went to bed that night and we were both tossing and turning, not getting a wink of sleep. Suddenly, Harry sat up in bed and whispered:

"'Are you awake, love?'

"I said: 'I am.'

"He said: 'I can't do it, I can't leave Sooty in the case.'

"I was so relieved. 'I'm very glad you said that, I haven't been able to sleep either for thinking about him.'

"So Harry decided: 'Tomorrow morning, I'll get him and take him with us. After all, he has paid for the trip.'

"Harry was right — Sooty had paid for it. So we took him on holiday."

On another family vacation, they had been travelling for nearly half an hour when the car suddenly screeched to a halt.

"I can't go without him, I can't go without him," cried Harry.

"What do you mean?" said Marjorie, "both the boys are in the back."

"No, not the boys," exclaimed Harry. "Sooty! I can't leave him at home. We'll have to go back and get him."

So they promptly turned back and thereafter Sooty always went on holiday with them. "The only drawback," says Marjorie, "was that people would see Harry and immediately ask: 'Have you got Sooty with you?' and Harry would have to do an impromptu show. If he hadn't been careful, he could have spent the entire holiday doing Sooty. But he loved it really."

The Corbetts always treated Sooty as if he really was a little boy. To them, he was far more than an inanimate lump of fur. "We couldn't have kept it going all those years if we hadn't thought of him as a real person," admits Marjorie. "I know it sounds silly, but to us he was always part of the family. He was a child to Harry and I. And I never thought about there being more than one Sooty, even though there was a pile of them in Harry's storeroom. Not only did we never, ever lay him on his face but he even travelled in a box with airholes so he could breathe properly. Only last year, I had to put a bit of tape on the bottom of Sooty's glove so that Harry could hang him up and I apologised to him. I said: 'I'm sorry, Sooty, but I've got to put this needle through you.' It's just my way."

Having conquered the British market, Harry was determined to make Sooty international. He visualised the golden bear being just as big in Hollywood as Blackpool. By chance, Walt Disney had just started a new American TV series called *The Mouseketeers* with Mickey Mouse and his friends and he wanted an act to give it an international flavour. The Disney representative in London, Perce Pearce, was contacted and asked whether there was anything on British television that might fit the bill. Pearce immediately thought of Sooty. "I've got the very thing," he told Disney. "It's a real cracker, it's number one — a teddy bear puppet." Disney was singularly unimpressed and wrote back saying he didn't think Sooty sounded suitable. Pearce would not be thwarted and asked Harry for a sample film which he promptly sent to Disney. The great man wrote back immediately and said, "book him." The deal was £12,000 for forty six-minute black and white films. But before he even came to make the first one, Harry received a nasty shock.

"I arrived at Perce Pearce's London office for the first day of filming, to be greeted by one of his colleagues. 'Haven't you heard the news? Perce had a heart attack last night. He's dead.' I was absolutely shattered. Perce had handled everything from Disney's point of view and he had all the ideas in his head. Nobody else there knew a thing about it. It was like a bad dream. Finally we found someone in a position of authority but I don't think he even knew who Sooty was. When we got round to starting filming, he just said: 'Right. What are we going to do?'"

The films were made in a tiny studio at St. John's Wood and this different medium presented an unexpected problem for Harry, who was used to doing everything live. When it came for Sooty to break an egg over Harry's head, instead of it being finished in one go, they did no fewer than four takes to get it absolutely right. So poor Harry had to endure this undignified treatment time after time. And at the end of each take, he had to wash his hair.

Harry should have made a lot of money out of the Disney films. But he didn't. For even the redoubtable Pearl Beresford was outgunned on this occasion. Harry reflected: "Pearl wasn't too hot on that deal. Disney wanted sole rights but Pearl should have insisted that we retained some interest. She should have stuck out. In the end, it became a take it or leave it situation. Pearl said: 'You've got to cash in on this, Harry, because it can't last.' She was convinced Sooty couldn't go on much longer. In fact, after she had been with me five years, there was a slight lull and she left. She said cheerio — as far as she was concerned, that was the end of Sooty. But it was really only the beginning.

"So Disney got the sole rights — I got nothing other than the original £12,000. The films were shown coast to coast in America and were repeated at least once. A friend told me he'd seen the shows in Hong Kong and when we were on holiday in places like Scandinavia, people would tell us they'd seen Sooty on TV there too. I didn't know a thing about it. I believe Disney also exported them to Canada and Australia. After all, he could sell them anywhere he pleased. It wasn't Disney's fault but a lot of that money should have been mine."

The shows went down very well in the States and Sooty soon built up a following of American fans. Shortly after the Disney enterprise, the Corbett family were on holiday in Majorca when the U.S. Fleet docked. "I was minding my own business in the bar," said Harry, "when an American sailor approached me with a puzzled expression on his face.

"'Excuse me,' he asked. 'You're not Sooty?'

"'Yes, that's right,' I said, 'I do Sooty.'

"'Gee fellas,' he shouted to his mates, 'this is little Sooty. Wait until I tell my kids back in Texas that I've met Sooty.'

"So we got chatting and this guy, Dave his name was, offered to take my sons David and Peter on a guided tour of his destroyer the next morning, which was the last day of our holiday. 'Just bring 'em along, I'll get them on board,' he promised. Well he didn't leave us until three in the morning and he was pretty drunk then and he and his pals were heading off for the centre of Palma. Anyway, later that morning, I took the boys to his ship and there at the top of the gangway was this Dave standing next to the commanding officer. Dave must have come straight from his booze-up to report on duty because although he was upright, he was completely unconscious. He was standing there, almost in a coma. We looked at him — nothing. He didn't recognise us at all. I explained to the officer with him that one of his men had invited us on board.

"'Which one?' he asked.

"I said: 'Oh not to worry. . .'

"'It doesn't matter which one, come on board anyway,' he said. So the boys got their trip round a U.S. destroyer — but it was no thanks to Sooty's newest fan!"

Despite the bitterness over the Disney affair, Harry was still set on taking America by storm. "I wanted Sooty to be as big as Mickey Mouse." Harry's new commercial manager Peter Barker put him in touch with one Mitchell J. Hamilburg, the multi-millionaire behind *Captain Kangaroo*, the long-running American children's show that went out every day of the year. "I went out to New York and did a show for Mitchell J. Hamilburg who was very impressed.

"'Tell me, Harry, how many shows can you do with this Sooty? One a day?'

"'One a day! No. More like one a week.'

"'That wouldn't even scratch the surface,' he said. With *Captain Kangaroo*, he was used to churning out shows like a sausage machine.

"'Harry, you could make a few million out of Sooty but you've got to come and live in the States for several years and devote your entire life to it. You have to decide if you think it's worth it.'

"I just left it like that and it never came to fruition."

"I'm very glad that it didn't," says Marjorie, "because it would have killed him."

Meanwhile, Harry had resolved to invest the £24,000 he had earned from the Disney and Oxo deals in a Bradford toy shop. "I thought very carefully about the future, as I had to with a family to support, and came to the conclusion that I should put the money into something for kiddies involving Sooty. A toy shop seemed the ideal solution. It was in North Parade, Bradford, and was generally reckoned to be just about the best toy shop in the north of England. While I was away doing television and summer seasons, Marjorie looked after the shop. She loved it, but while it was very exciting, it also created a headache for me because I was trying to write scripts, do the show and run a business, all at the same time. The problem with owning a toy shop is that the interest is only really seasonal — all around Christmas. We soon realised we could never succeed on toys alone, so we decided to try and grab the kiddies before they were born by selling maternity wear too. Therefore we bought the shop two doors up. There was a cleaner's in-between but our two premises met upstairs above the cleaner's and we knocked the wall through so that they formed one large shop. We sold some beautiful items, but business-wise the whole venture was disappointing. We needed to make £28,000 a year to break even, which was a lot of money in the late Fifties, but we never quite made it. Unfortunately, the area we were in went downhill rapidly and a lot of the surrounding shops moved into the centre of Bradford, so trade suffered. I eventually sold it after seven years and to be honest, I was glad to be rid of it. It turned out to be a big mistake — I only wish I'd bought a larger house instead and invested my money in property rather than a business."

The year of 1957 heralded a major landmark in the story of Sooty — the arrival of a melancholy-faced hound who would do anything for a pound of chipolatas. It was of course Sweep. By that time, Harry had begun to run out of magic (probably due to a world shortage of Oofle Dust) and wanted to steer the show more in the direction of situation comedy. He wanted to expand, to bring in new sets and a partner in crime for Sooty. "I saw a drawing of a spaniel with long black ears and its paws spread out on the front cover of *London Opinion* magazine. It looked most appealing and I immediately thought: 'That's it.' So I sent it to Chad Valley and asked them to make a puppet like it. They sent one back but it was hopeless — it looked really peculiar. Marjorie and I had to sit down and completely alter the expression, giving him droopy eyebrows and a droopy mouth. And so Sweep was born, the name being a natural progression from soot. We decided that Sweep should be four, a year younger than Sooty, and would be as thick as a brick, the sort who always gets the wrong end of the stick. To put it kindly, Sweep is dim. For the first two years, I operated Sooty and Sweep, one on each hand, but then I asked my brother Leslie if he was interested in taking over Sweep."

Leslie had already assisted his brother on an earlier programme. "Harry had decided he wanted to demonstrate his piano playing," says Leslie, "so he devised a show where he could play the piano and push Sooty to one side and say: 'This is my bit, you're out of it.' While Harry was performing Chopin's "Revolutionary Study", which is an extremely technical piece, he needed Sooty to keep coming in and interrupt by shutting the lid on Harry's fingers and getting up to all his usual mischief. Obviously, Harry couldn't do everything so he asked me to work Sooty. I remember this was when Liberace was at his height and his trademark was a candelabra on the piano, so Bill Garrett made a special Sooty-sized candelabra. And that was the start of my involvement with the show."

Shortly afterwards, Leslie joined Harry on a regular basis. Since the shows were then made in Manchester not London, Leslie was able to get time off work from his job with the Electricity Board in Bradford to travel the forty-odd miles. "I spent most of my holidays with Sweep," says Leslie. "We didn't get overtime with the Electricity Board, we had to take time in lieu, so I was more or less able to take a day off whenever I wanted it. The shows were always done on a Sunday, which was quite convenient as far as I was concerned and we used to drive over in the morning, rehearse, do the show in the afternoon and return to Guiseley. Mind you, there were times when we nearly didn't make it, struggling across the Pennines in thick snow. It was always a bit dodgy because we could go over in fine weather and by the time we'd finished there'd be a foot or more of snow. I often had to bounce up and down in the back of the car to keep it going."

Leslie had no previous experience of puppeteering but, like Harry, he had large, flexible hands so Sweep was never hunched up like a canine Quasimodo. Leslie's very presence meant that Harry now had one hand free to do other business with Sooty. Sometimes Leslie worked Sooty and Sweep, which enabled Harry to expand the show enormously. "If I did both puppets, I used to do Sooty with my right hand and Sweep with my left," says Leslie. "This created a problem since I am very much right-handed and anyway the puppets were made for a right hand. In fact, they were so uncomfortable on the left that eventually Harry had to have some left-handed Sweeps specially made for me. I was very much a behind-the-scenes man and I was only ever seen on screen once — that was as a Santa Claus with a reet broad Yorkshire accent in *Sooty's Christmas Dream*. Because people only saw Harry, they couldn't understand how he managed to do so much. They used to say to him: 'You've got Sooty here and Sweep there and you've still got another hand. How do you do it?' It never occurred to them to ask who was doing Sweep. I think many people were convinced Harry had three arms!"

Harry was full of praise for his brother's contribution. "Les was a natural. The great thing was we had the same sense of humour and used to roll around helpless with laughter thinking up ideas for the show. After doing the programme, we would pop into the pub for a drink and the conversation always ended up being about what Sooty and Sweep were going to get up to next."

Leslie adds: "I've often said that Sooty and Sweep themselves wrote quite a lot of the scripts because Harry and I would sit down with the puppets on and just take it from there, reacting to each other."

Leslie quickly became as devoted to Sweep as Harry was to Sooty. "Sooty was part of Harry," says Leslie, "and when I started doing Sweep, the same thing happened to me. I got so involved with the character that if Sweep got a face full of custard, I ducked too. I think Sweep and I have similar personalities — I'm something of an underdog too. Also I love sausages, although I must admit I'm not too keen on bones."

It was Leslie who was responsible for Sweep's distinctive voice. "Originally, inside the puppet was a bag containing a metal reed," says Leslie, "and when pressed this would make Sweep's squeaky bark. Once we were doing a programme with Sooty and Sweep in the bathroom — Sooty was in the bath and Sweep was having a shower. We rehearsed it dry until, on the final run-through, we used water. I said to the studio hands: 'Make sure the water isn't stone cold, would you?' Well when it came out, you could have boiled an egg in it. I was scalded, but it was even worse for Sweep. He was soaked and his voice bag simply fell apart. There was no way it would work and we had no spares so in desperation I suggested: 'Why don't we cut the metal reed out of the bag and I'll see if I can blow it?' I found that not only could I produce his familiar bark but I could make other noises too. I could even make it sound as if he was singing — out of tune, of course. It went down a bomb and we kept it like that from then on."

Together, Sooty with his magic wand and his spells of "Izzy Whizzy, Let's Get Busy" and Sweep with his endless strings of sausages, were a formidable double act. They became the Morecambe and Wise of glove puppets. Some people preferred Sweep to Sooty. A woman once sidled up to Harry in a pub and confided: "Ooh, I do think that Sweep's sexy!" And Harry recalled being accosted by a cluster of archetypal flat-capped Yorkshiremen chanting: "We want Sweep. We want Sweep." Harry didn't have him at the time and with more than an iota of bluntness replied: "Oh, bugger Sweep!" Leslie confirms: "Lots of children preferred Sweep to Sooty, who was a bit bombastic, bossy even. I remember Barney Colehan once calling him 'a bumptious little bear.'" It certainly requires a forceful personality to be bossy without ever opening your mouth. . .

Harry's postman wasn't too sure about the newcomer, however. He could never understand why a parcel he regularly delivered to the Corbetts made a strange noise until he discovered it was a consignment of spare squeakers for Sweep.

In spite of Harry's personal setbacks with Disney and the toy shop, Sooty's progress continued unabated. Along with roast beef, the Mini and Churchill, he had become a British institution, loved by people of all ages. Fortunately for Harry, this included the police who, on more than one occasion, overlooked his misdemeanours. Once, he was stopped by a patrol for speeding but was allowed to proceed when he explained that he had only exceeded the limit because Sooty was late for rehearsals! Another time, Harry was convinced that he and Sooty would end up before the magistrates. "We were driving along when a police motorcyclist suddenly roared past and pulled up in front of us. I knew for a fact that my brakes weren't working properly, I'd just overshot a red light and to make matters worse I'd nearly knocked him off his bike as he slowed down to stop us. He came over to us and got his book out.

"I thought: 'Here we go, I'm for it now —

I'm going to be done for about half a dozen things.'

"The policeman said: 'I'm very sorry, sir, to have to use my uniform and stop you in this manner but I recognised you as you went past and my kid would never forgive me if I didn't get your autograph.' And he handed me his book to sign.

"I breathed a huge sigh of relief. 'Of course you can, officer. Of course you can, with the greatest of pleasure.'"

Not everyone wanted to be associated with Sooty though. The little bear hit the headlines again in the early Sixties when Jarrow councillors vigorously protested about Sooty being chosen to open the town's new shopping centre. They decreed that Sooty lacked dignity and they wanted someone of far greater standing to perform the act. "The developers must think we're a lot of goons," moaned one councillor. However great his inner hurt, Sooty, as ever, maintained a noble silence. Eventually, the councillors saw the error of their ways and Harry and Sooty were welcomed with open arms although it was to an informal, rather than the formal, opening of the centre.

Gilbert Harding wasn't too sure what to make of Sooty either. The son of a policeman, Harding was known as "the rudest man in Britain" for his appalling behaviour as a panellist on *What's My Line*? He made front page news when he argued with chairman Eamonn Andrews (in fact, the pair were great friends and their rows were rigged to boost the ratings), any challengers who were unwittingly evasive or who, in Harding's opinion, possessed an inadequate command of the English language, or on one celebrated occasion with Peter Brough's famous dummy Archie Andrews. There aren't too many people who could argue with a piece of wood in front of ten million viewers! Harry was the mystery guest on a 1960 edition of *What's My Line*? and, after failing to beat the panel, he took Sooty in his hat to meet them. He recounted:"When we got to Gilbert Harding, Sooty whispered in my ear. I said: 'What do you mean, who's this? It's Gilbert Harding. . . You've never heard of him? You must have heard of Gilbert Harding.' I tried to make Sooty as intrigued by Gilbert as Gilbert was by Sooty but it was all a bit above Gilbert's head. He just sat there curling up with this bloody bear looking at him. He didn't know what to say or do." The following morning's *Daily Mail* reported Harding's "hideous embarrassment" at meeting Sooty. It continued: "He was at a loss to know how to talk to it. He couldn't go along with the fantasy. To him, it was just a lump of cloth on someone's hand."

"Immediately after me, Bill Garrett came on and actually beat the panel," said Harry. "His official occupation was 'Sooty's prop maker' but the panel only got as far as 'the man who makes Sooty puppets'. So Bill got a certificate which was his pride and joy. He was chuffed to hell."

As Sooty's fame spread to places like Germany, Gibraltar, Hungary, Italy and Nigeria, his show remained so popular in Britain that on Christmas Day 1964 it actually attracted more viewers in the London area than either *Z Cars* or *Coronation Street*. But Harry was never one to rest on his laurels. He wanted to expand further and set about introducing a third character to join Sooty and Sweep. But even he couldn't have known the furore it would arouse.

CHAPTER THREE

SEX AND THE SINGLE BEAR

By 1964, Harry had come to the conclusion that *The Sooty Show* needed a character with a voice. But what sort of animal should it be? At the time, the biggest attraction at London Zoo was Chi Chi the giant panda, so Harry thought of introducing a little black and white panda called Soo, a name which was suitably oriental and also an abbreviation of Sooty. "I just wanted a little girlfriend for Sooty. After all, every child has a little pal and they walk along holding hands. There was nothing more to it than that, it was all perfectly innocent.

"So I told Trevor Hill, who was our producer then, that I wanted to introduce a new character.

"'Oh yes. Good,' he said. 'What is it?'

"'I want to bring in a girl-friend for Sooty.'

"'No. Sorry. We can't do that.'

"'Why not?'

"'That's sex creeping into the programme.'

"'You're joking, Trevor.'

"'I'm not.'

"'You must be. How can you have sex with a teddy bear puppet and his little friend from next door?'

"He was insistent. 'It will create bad feeling and it's not right. I'm not condoning it. The answer's no, you can't do it.'

"I said I can't believe it but if you say no,

I'll have to forget it. And I did, until about a year later when I was playing at a theatre in Wimbledon and a chap by the name of Doug McDonald, a reporter on the *Daily Mail*, started chatting to me.

"He said: 'Things are very quiet at the moment and I'm desperate for a story. Is there anything new in Sooty?'

"I said, 'There's not now but there was going to be a year ago. I wanted to bring in a girlfriend for Sooty but the BBC said no — the producer said it was sex creeping in.'

"This guy's face lit up. 'Is that true?' he asked.

"'Absolutely, ring Trevor Hill if you like.'

"I don't know whether he did or not but the next day the papers were full of stories with headlines like 'No Sex For Sooty'. Every paper from *The Times* down carried it. Jean Rook of the *Daily Express* later told me that Fleet Street had never known anything like it, the whole place went completely mad because it was such a great story — the world's best-loved children's puppet being linked with sex.

"Anyway, the story ran and ran and eventually got quite embarrassing. The BBC rang me up:

"'Have you got a vendetta against us?' they asked. 'Remember, there's a contract on a new Sooty series hanging fire and if there's one more word about Soo and sex, the contract will be cancelled.'

"'It's not my fault,' I protested.

"A week after the original story, Doug McDonald came back to me and said: 'In view of the millions of pounds worth of publicity you've just had, have you decided to go ahead with Soo? You must insist on doing it now. Have you told the BBC that unless they agree to it, you won't do any more programmes?'

"I said: 'Certainly not.'

"'Well,' he persisted, 'can I say that if they

won't let you do it, you won't do any more programmes?'

"'No, you can't say that.' But he did. In the following morning's paper, there was the story: 'Harry Corbett Gives Ultimatum to BBC — no Soo, no show.'

"I thought that would make relations even worse with the BBC but again I protested my innocence and the whole thing was smoothed over so that Soo could finally make her bow. I think because of all the publicity, the whole country was waiting to see Soo and the BBC was really left with little option. But they did lay down one condition — Sooty and Soo were not allowed to touch!"

So Harry managed to get his own way and Soo teamed up with the boys in a menage a trois. Certainly for somebody who was supposed to live next door, she spent an awful lot of time at The Sooteries. But she always kept her fur on. With Harry manipulating Sooty and Leslie in charge of Sweep, Marjorie was the obvious choice for Soo, particularly now that she was no longer involved in running the ill-fated toy shop. There was just one problem. Marjorie didn't have the finger stretch of the men so the puppet would have looked decidedly contorted on her hand. Not for the first time, the solution was provided by the incomparable Bill Garrett who built an artificial hand on a stick which Marjorie held from below to operate the head, arms and body. Because she was on a stick, Soo was more sophisticated than the straightforward glove puppets and was able to move her body and head independently. "This meant she was able to keep her head still and look at Sooty but exit with a lovely little wiggle," enthused Harry, perhaps aware that he had created a miniature sex symbol after all.

By talking from the back of her throat, Marjorie gave Soo a breathless high-pitched voice, a remarkable achievement since her own voice is deep enough to have once played the Peggy Mount role in a stage production of *Sailor Beware*! Marjorie also made all the characters' clothes. "If Sooty and Sweep were soldiers, it was me who used to make their uniforms, right down to the bearskins and chinstraps. Everything was as near to the real thing as I could make it. I used to work in a shop that made ladies' dresses but I wasn't allowed to touch them. I could do embroidery but I couldn't make a dress to save my life. Yet I coped with Soo, although it was very difficult to make her clothes sufficiently different in such a small size. So I found shops that sold bits and pieces of material, like a quarter of a yard, and bought from them. People thought I was mad — they were intrigued as to why I needed all those oddments. I must have made over three hundred dresses for Soo, including the special ones that were cut short at the knee so you could see her little legs when she was playing the piano. I thought nothing of working on them until the early hours of the morning — they were a real labour of love. If Harry had married someone who hadn't a clue about a needle and thread, I just don't know what he would have done."

It wasn't only when buying oddments of cloth that Harry and Marjorie mystified shopkeepers. Harry vividly remembered going into an anglers' shop in Bradford to order a complete new fishing rod.

"The shopowner said: 'Certainly, sir. How many sections would you like?'

"'Two, please.'

"'Do you want an expensive reel?'

"'Yes and all the trimmings. It's got to be really professional.'

"'How long would you like it to be overall, sir?'

"'Eighteen inches.'

"'What did you say? Eighteen inches?'

"He couldn't take it in, then he had another look at my face and said: 'You're not that Sooty fellow, are you? Is this for Sooty? In which case, that will be a pleasure, sir. '"

Marjorie adds: "I've often felt a pillock

going into shops and people asking what it's for. I went into a butcher's once and asked for four foot of sausages. The butcher did a double take before sternly informing me:

"'Madam, we sell sausages by the pound not by the yard. Anyway, why do you want that length?'

"I said: 'It's for Sweep — they're his Christmas decorations. . .'"

In addition to Soo, Harry introduced some other colourful new characters during this period. "One of my favourites was Butch, a tough dog with a great personality. We were doing a programme where Sooty was a boxing champion and because we didn't want to him to fight his best friend Sweep, we had this fierce-looking dog specially made. Then there was Algernon Fortescue the talking parrot and we also felt we needed a cat so I came up with Kipper, who got his name because he was always dozing off. Bill Garrett made a special fibreglass puppet with a bulb in the tummy and whenever the bulb was squeezed, Kipper closed his eyes. But he never really took off — he simply wasn't photogenic enough, he didn't look good on screen. And we had good old Ramsbottom the snake who we brought in for a show about snake-charming. Originally, he was going to be called Fanshaw and have a posh Oxford accent but then Leslie tried it out in broad Yorkshire and it worked a treat. He caught on to such an extent that a Ramsbottom Appreciation Society was formed in Cheshire and they complained vigorously when he wasn't on the show one week, even threatening to take legal action if he wasn't back soon!"

That Sooty and his pals were around at all was more by luck than judgment after their world was nearly wrecked in a serious fire at the warehouse near Leeds where Harry stored all the show's props. It started through a faulty heater, next to a cupboard housing tins of paint. The paint went up in flames, causing £10,000 worth of damage, the biggest casualty being a marvellous new set that Bill Garrett had just completed, the centrepiece of which was an electric organ. "Not only did the fire nearly destroy the warehouse, it nearly destroyed me," revealed Harry. "I was just about to leave to do a personal appearance in Skipton when I got the phone call telling me the warehouse was on fire. I dashed over but there was nothing much I could do. I was terribly upset, it was a huge shock to my system. I felt like giving up there and then. I thought: 'I can't start all over again.' Bill's lovely set was ruined, but fortunately the fire didn't get through to all the other props otherwise I could have been finished. And when the brigade had finally put it out and water was lying everywhere, a photographer from the *Bradford Telegraph and Argus* had the nerve to come up to me and ask:

"'Could you find a smouldered Sooty and pose in the middle of the debris?'

"I could have killed him, it was so heartless. I said: 'Do you want me to say cheese as well. . . ?'"

Under the headline 'Sooty and Sweep Cheat Death', the press reported that the puppets were badly singed but unhurt.

From the arduous days of the Butlin's summer season, Harry had put on special stage shows during the school holidays, especially at Christmas. The rest of the year had been limited to television and the charity work he did for the National Children's Home. But then Harry conceived an idea that would enable him to do stage shows the whole year round. "I thought why don't I put on shows in term time as well, just after the kids have finished school, at around 4.30? That would still leave the theatre free to put on a play or whatever in the evening." Harry took his suggestion to the Grade agency, who were handling his affairs at the time, but they said it would never work — nobody would be able to see a puppet the size of a glove on the stage of a large theatre. Then another theatrical agent, Vincent Shaw, met Harry at a party and offered to help.

It took Vincent Shaw three months to fix up

Talented brothers — Harry on accordion and Les on sax

Harry and Marjorie's wedding day, 1944

Sweep — bone idol

Soo, the femme fatale banned by the BBC for introducing sex to the show

Butch — Rotweiller of the Sixties

An early Sooty puppet — he improved with age

Sooty operates Bill Garrett's ingenious sausage making machine while Sweep surveys juicy steaks in the days before Mad Cow Disease

Peace at last — Sooty counts sheep and Sweep counts sausages

Sooty tries to work out which of the Beverley Sisters is Billy Wright

Sooty goes to bed — this was Harry's favourite routine, although you wouldn't think so from that famous expression

OUCH! Sooty hammers home a point to poor Harry

Harry probably suffered more in the cause of his art than any other performer. Here Sooty helps him to test whether his shirt is drip-dry

The 1956 television commercial for Oxo. It gives a meal bear appeal

The police had to control the crowds when Sooty's toy shop opened in Bradford

The boys at the organ — and Harry had a hand in it too

the first date, simply because then there was no precedent for doing children's stage shows at any time other than the school holidays. But he stuck at it and eventually booked *The Sooty Show* into the Theatre Royal, York, for a week. "From Wednesday onwards, there wasn't a seat to be had," said Harry.

"I thought: 'This is marvellous.'"

"Vincent Shaw said: 'Shall I book some more for you?'

"'Get the winter filled in, we'll go on a provincial tour.' And within a week, he came back with a full list of venues.

"After York, the second on the list was the Rose Theatre, Harrogate, and it's fair to say that if that had been the first one, we wouldn't have done any more — I'd have said to Marj: 'Forget it.' It was a complete disaster. The theatre was mucky and they hadn't done any publicity, so business was diabolical. But having done York, we knew it could work so we persevered with the tour.

"It was great fun touring — we used to call it our circus. We started off with all the props in a horse box towed by Marjorie's car while I towed the caravan that was our home for months on end." Marjorie says: "We still get Christmas cards from people on whose drives we parked the caravan all those years ago."

And nobody ever moaned that they couldn't see little Sooty on stage, although a woman sitting at the back of the circle in an eighteen hundred seater theatre at Cardiff did once call the manager to complain.

"What is it, madam?" he inquired.

"It's Sooty," she said. "I can't hear a word he's saying to Mr. Corbett."

"I'll go and tell him, madam," replied the manager, patiently.

When the story was duly related to Harry, he said: "Go and tell her neither can I!"

Sooty was a huge box office attraction

throughout Britain. The ninety-minute stage show required no scenery, only curtains, and theatres frequently took more from Sooty in the afternoon than from their evening productions. Harry said: "Often on tour we used to bump into actors from Shakespearean plays in the same town as us. They wanted to know why we were doing better business, why people preferred Sooty to *A Midsummer Night's Dream*."

Harry's stage shows reminded him, not that he ever needed it, that children can usually be relied upon to provide the most embarrassing answers. They are so brutally honest. He remembered an encounter on Blackpool pier, where the whole Sooty story had begun many years earlier, with a little lad aged about seven. "He had got to the stage where, rather like children are with Father Christmas, he wasn't sure whether Sooty was real or not.

"'Hello mister,' he said.

"'Hello,' said I. 'Have you seen the show?'

"'Yes.'

"'Did you like it?'

"'Yes, smashing. But I know what you do, mister.'

"'What's that?' said I, not knowing what to expect.

"'You put your hand up Sooty's bottom.'"

For twenty-three years from 1966, Sooty was an annual Christmas attraction at the Mayfair Theatre, off London's Piccadilly — a feat which has earned him a place in the Guinness Book of Records for the longest run of consecutive Christmas seasons at the same theatre. (He also holds the record for the most durable TV show — thirty-eight years to date). Harry regularly used to hold talent contests at the Mayfair.

"I got one lad up on stage and asked him: 'What do you want to be when you grow up?'

"'A bugler,' he answered.

"'Oh, what does your daddy do? Does he

play the bugle?'

"'No. He chisels numbers on gravestones!'"

Harry would have received a somewhat different reply had he asked another young contestant about his father's occupation. "Marjorie used to pick the children for the talent show out of the audience, but when she came to choose a bright lad named George, she didn't see his mother because she had her back to her. I nearly said to this George: 'What does your father do?' but for some reason I didn't. George was going to sing "Away in a Manger" and I had an accordion handy to accompany him.

"I said cheerfully: 'Would you like me to play the accordion while you sing?'

"'No thank you,' he replied matter-of-factly. He obviously didn't want me ruining his song! Anyway, he sang beautifully and was a clear winner so he was given his prize, a Sooty puppet. When I got to the wings, somebody said: 'Do you know who you just got up? It was the Duchess of Kent's lad.' You could have knocked me down. But it was really smashing that I didn't know who he was, because for a start nobody could claim the whole thing was rigged and also it meant that the Duchess of Kent had been able to bring her son along and enjoy *The Sooty Show* like any other family. And they must have liked it because we saw them buying six puppets from the foyer on the way out."

Vincent Shaw was only too aware of the value of publicity, but he faced a difficult job persuading Harry. "He wouldn't co-operate at all on publicity," says Shaw. "He couldn't see the point of it. Quite simply, he was the best amateur in the business — and I don't think he ever really wanted to be a professional. I remember dropping in to the Mayfair and him telling me about picking the Duchess of Kent's son.

"I said: 'Have you told the papers?'

"'Why should I?' asked Harry, bemused.

"I said: 'For Christ's sake. . .' and rushed

back to the office and we made the front page the next day. But it would never have occurred to Harry to tell anybody."

Inevitably, the increased workload involved with mounting nationwide tours meant that Harry was unable to devote quite as much time to doing shows for the National Children's Home. In 1958, one hundred thousand registered Sooty fans had each subscribed 1s 6d a year to the National Children's Home and for ten years Harry travelled the length and breadth of the country on charity work, raising thousands of pounds.

"Each year they gave me a list with hundreds of venues on it and I would do as many as humanly possible. It was my big charity effort. I used to do my favourite Sooty routine of all, Sooty goes to bed, where I read him a story, hear him say his prayers for the children, tuck him into bed with his hot water bottle and give him a goodnight kiss. And all the kiddies, who had been shouting and cheering earlier in the show, had to tiptoe out of the theatre in complete silence in case they woke him up. For three years I did a special Christmas party at the Cumberland Hotel near Marble Arch and the only noise that could be heard was the waitresses clearing away the plates and cutlery. It was an amazing sight, adults who saw it for the first time couldn't believe I could keep an entire audience of raucous children spellbound in silence for so long.

"I did one NCH show in the most unlikely of venues — the pulpit of a church. The routine I did that day was extremely complicated and involved a real mouse in a silver dish as well as some coins and glasses. I set it all up myself but because I had to dash off somewhere else, I asked whether someone could dismantle it for me after the show. I emphasised that since there was glassware and a live mouse, it had to be done very carefully. Sure enough when the performance had finished and I was getting ready to leave, this chap started to take the apparatus down. He made a right mess of it — he couldn't have done it worse if he'd tried. His arms and legs were everywhere and the whole lot, glasses, coins and mouse, collapsed in a heap. I found the mouse huddled in the corner with the silver dish on top of it. When I recounted the story to my brother Les, he said: 'I bet the mouse thought "That's showbusiness."'

"But the touring made it much more difficult to do the NCH shows, one of the reasons being that most theatres had a clause in the contract stating that you couldn't do another show within a twenty-mile radius. When I was at the Palace Theatre in Cambridge Circus, the theatre's boss Emile Littler wouldn't allow Sooty to appear at Westminster Central Hall for the National Children's Home. He said the Hall held three thousand and claimed that if people went to see Sooty there, they wouldn't come to see the show at the Palace. It was absolute nonsense — the show at Westminster would have been far smaller than the one at the Palace and anyway I'd have reminded the audience: 'Don't forget to come and see Sooty at the Palace Theatre.'

"Emile Littler was a hard nut though, a real dictator. In fact, I always thought Littler was short for Little Hitler! I remember I was doing a Christmas show at the Palace and I was supposed to be at a meeting with Littler and his entourage. But I'd been out on the town the night before and had overslept. My slumbers were suddenly interrupted by a phone call from his secretary demanding to know why I wasn't at this meeting. Like everyone else, I was terrified of Littler so I got dressed in record time and rushed to the meeting. I walked in and mumbled an apology but Littler just scowled at me. The atmosphere was decidedly tense until he accidentally knocked something off his desk. As he went round and bent down to pick it up, his trousers split from top to bottom and we were left with this bare bum facing us. We fell about laughing and Littler's pomposity was squashed on the spot.

"But the upshot of the attitude of Littler and other impressarios was that my work for the National

Children's Home began to fall through as they realised they could no longer have me on tap. It was a shame because I loved working for them."

Harry's other major charity work was via the Sooty and Sweep collecting boxes for the Royal National Institute for the Blind which have become a feature of shop counters all over the country. "They approached me for permission," recalled Harry, "and naturally I said I'd be delighted and sent them a couple of puppets to model the boxes on. The very first one was installed in Princes Street, Edinburgh, in 1964 and was full within a week. There was a wonderful response. Nobody could believe the pulling-power of those two little puppets." Nowadays there are some fifty thousand Sooty and Sweep collecting boxes spread throughout the country and each year they raise the staggering total of £1 million.

Meanwhile, touring had become a family affair for the Corbetts with Harry and Marjorie being joined by their elder son David as stage manager and chief caravan-washer and with Peter also helping out occasionally. Since he had a full-time job, Leslie was mainly restricted to operating Sweep on television. Marjorie's presence in particular was a great comfort to Harry. Known to the rest of the family as "Tobes" (a nickname she was given by David because her beaming smile and ample proportions reminded him of a Toby jug) her boundless enthusiasm even rivalled that of Harry. "I used to call her Atom Bomb," laughed Harry, "because she was such a bundle of energy in those days. And her personality shone through on stage, along with her undoubted skill."

A typical example of Marjorie's resilience and determination was the time when she carried on with the show with flames lapping around her ankles. "We were doing a show featuring a rocket launch," she recalls, "and we used real fireworks. All I had to do was take a clean Sooty off Harry's hand when he reached down and put a sooty Sooty on to make it look as if he'd had an accident. I was lying on a sheet to stop me getting too filthy with my dirty Sooty at the ready, but as the rocket was launched and all the fireworks went off, gunpowder started dripping down on to the sheet like hot fat and it caught fire. So I'm there holding this blackened Sooty, trying to get the clean puppet off Harry with one hand, trying to give him the dirty one and all the time putting bloody flames out and making sure that I didn't catch fire as well. Meanwhile, the show just went on. . ."

Marjorie was soon to need all her courage when, during one tour, she was struck down by diabetes. "I was in a really bad way — at first they didn't know what was wrong with me. I came up with skin like an elephant, all over my arms, legs and feet. Thank goodness it didn't hit my face because, although I didn't appear much in front of the public then, I wouldn't have been able to do the show. It was a very trying time, because I was in agony and had great difficulty walking across the stage without it showing. So I just had to hobble on, gird my loins like an old soldier and try to last out. Sometimes it made me feel so sick I had to operate Soo with a bucket by my side. . . just in case."

Harry and Marjorie were both performers of the "old school", epitomising that indomitable Windmill spirit that says no matter what, the show must go on. It was a dedication that at times bordered on downright stubbornness, but there was no way they were ever going to disappoint Sooty's loyal fans. Once, despite severe back pains, Marjorie steadfastly refused to go to hospital until the discomfort became so great that Harry finally managed to persuade her to seek medical help. There, surgeons discovered an abcess the size of an orange in her pelvis. Still undaunted, she insisted on recording Soo's voice from her hospital bed. On another occasion Harry did the Christmas show in agony after falling down the stairs at home and cracking a rib.

Harry also had a close encounter at the Leicester Square Theatre when he unwittingly flicked cigarette ash on some gun cotton. The cotton exploded and scalded his valuable hands. "It could have been much worse," he reflected. "If I had been leaning over at the time, I would have lost my eyes. And that would have been the end of Sooty."

David Corbett began helping his father as a schoolboy. During the holidays, he would pass him the props for the TV shows. "It was all live so I was scared stiff in case I handed him the wrong things." As stage manager, he was also responsible for setting up the props and he remembers a summer season in a booth on Blackpool pier that provided one of Harry's most humiliating moments. "Among Sooty's regular support acts was a children's magician named Ernest Radford, known to all as Uncle Ernest. He was a wonderful entertainer and one day my father and I were so enthralled watching his act that we completely forgot about Sooty and Sweep. When Uncle Ernest finished, he introduced Uncle Harry and Sooty but the set was blank. We weren't ready. Worse still, lying on top of the booth were the Sooty and Sweep puppets that my father had taken off while we were admiring Ernest. My father was dreadfully embarrassed about the children seeing the puppets lying around inanimate. It could have shattered their illusions."

Blessed with a highly inventive mind, Harry was forever thinking up new ideas for Sooty's stage shows — and this meant more headaches for the redoubtable Bill Garrett. After seeing the film *Around the World in Eighty Days*, Harry came up with a plan to put Sooty in a balloon, but it turned out to be something of a disaster. Harry ascertained that when filled with helium, a balloon five feet in diameter could carry between six and seven pounds in weight so he said to Bill: "I want a basket about seven inches square and six inches deep and I want it radio controlled so that Sooty can look over the side, wave to the audience and turn his head backwards and forwards. Get on with it!" As ever, Bill came up with an impeccable design which appeared foolproof until it was used for the very first time at the City Varieties, Leeds. Prior to the show, the balloon was duly inflated to five feet but it could barely lift itself off the floor, let alone a basket. Harry checked his information and was told that it shouldn't have been five feet in diameter, it should be five feet radius, making a ten foot diameter which was totally out of the question for a stage show. So after much discussion, they instead used a solid balloon of spun aluminium. The day before the show, Bill painstakingly tied it to the theatre beams but half-way through the performance there was a tremendous crash in the wings. The supporting rope had given way and the balloon was in ruins. Sooty would not be taking off that afternoon.

Bill Garrett was not a man who could accept failure, and Harry dreaded having to tell him what had happened. The saving grace was that Bill himself had been the one who had tied the balloon up. "Bill went white when I told him," said Harry. "I said: 'Look, I know I won't get the balloon back this week, Bill, but do your best.' At nine the next morning my phone rang. It was Bill. 'It's ready,' he said. He had worked right through the night, rebuilding the damn thing. And of course it worked perfectly."

Two regular companions of the Corbetts in those days were Geoff and Jean Richardson; they have remained close friends ever since. "I first met Harry back in 1948," says Geoff, "when he played the piano at the Royal Hotel, I!kley. I was also something of a pianist and we used to do the odd duet together. After that, I didn't see him for some years until one day I switched on the television and called to Jean in the kitchen: 'Come and look who's on the television — it's our pal from the Royal.' So we got in touch and the four of us used to socialise after that. Although the main thing Harry and I had in common was the piano, I was also very interested in Sooty and the magic. After a while, I acted as Harry's chauffeur and helped him a lot with his charity shows, setting up the props and so on.

"We even discussed the possibility of my becoming his manager. But I was the director of a textile company in Bradford with a reasonable amount of security and it only wanted one accident to Harry's right hand and the whole job would have been finished. So I declined the offer but I agreed to help him wherever I could with book-keeping and general administration."

The pair had some hair-raising times together when the chaos behind the cameras was often equal to that inflicted by Sooty in front of them. "I remember Harry ringing me in my office one Friday while he was down in London doing his Christmas show at the Palace Theatre. He said: 'I've got a live TV programme to do on Sunday and I've just realised I haven't done any preparation for it. I don't know what I'm going to do at all. Can you go to my storeroom and put anything in the car that's musical, bring it down to me and stay over and give me a hand with the show?' So I drove down in thick snow and arrived at Twickenham, where Harry was staying. We went for a drink and the pub was full of Welshmen as it was the eve of the England v. Wales rugby international. They immediately recognised Harry, there was a piano in the bar and the result was we didn't get any work done that evening. 'Never mind,' said Harry, 'we'll go to the Palace Theatre in the morning and rehearse till we get a show together.'

"So next morning we went to the Palace, but all the electrics had failed and workmen were hammering everywhere trying to fix them. It was impossible for us to rehearse there. Harry said, 'Not to worry, you go off to the match and afterwards we'll go to the Riverside Studios and we'll do it there.'

"We got to Riverside and were all set up

just about to start when this chap came in and said: 'You can't do that in here — *Dixon of Dock Green's* just going on in the next studio. There's to be no sound in here at all.' So we watched Dixon and went over the road and had a drink with the cast. Harry had also promised the Welsh boys that he'd be back at the Winning Post Hotel after the match, so we returned there for the rest of the evening. 'No problem,' he said, 'we'll go back to Riverside in the morning and rehearse until we've got a programme.'

"Once again, we were on the point of beginning at Riverside when suddenly the huge scenery doors were flung open to set up a new show. It was freezing cold and blowing a gale through the open doors so Harry said: 'Oh bugger this,' and we went to the canteen for a coffee. He sat down and came out with one of his prize remarks: 'You know Geoff, right now millions of children are thinking, 'I wonder what Sooty's going to be doing today.' Little do they know that we're sitting here thinking exactly the same!'

"Anyway, we finally got back into the studio and somehow managed to sort out a programme. When I arrived home in Yorkshire, a friend said: 'Were you helping Harry today, Geoff? Because it's the best show I've ever seen him do. . . '

"Harry had a habit of ringing me up for no apparent reason, just to have a chat. This might be at one o'clock lunch time or one in the morning. Once, he rang through to my office at about 10am and said:

"'I just thought I'd tell you what I'm doing. I'm lying in bed at the Grosvenor House Hotel, surrounded by the morning's newspapers and the sun is shining.'

"'Fine,' said I, 'and when are you setting off for Huddersfield?'

"'Why? What's on at Huddersfield?'

"'You're doing a show for the National Children's Home there tonight.'

"'No, it's tomorrow.'

"I said, 'No. It's tonight.'

"Harry was insistent. 'It's tomorrow.'

"'Harry,' I said, 'you are in Huddersfield at 7. 30 this evening.'

"'Just a minute. I know it's tomorrow but I'll get my diary.'

"There was a pregnant pause. . . 'Bloody hell!'

"So I hastily packed his stuff on the trailer, set it all up on the stage and met him at Huddersfield station. Fortunately the train arrived on time at two minutes past seven, we drove to the town hall and he walked straight on and did the show. Jean and I christened him 'violets' — we said if he fell down the loo, he'd come up smelling of violets."

But Harry wasn't smelling of violets when the Richardsons and the Corbetts went on holiday to the tulip fields of Holland. "Harry had just bought this very expensive mohair suit," says Geoff, "but while he was walking round the tulip fields, he fell in a dyke which was nothing more than an open sewer. There was Harry in his brand new mohair suit with one leg covered in sewage. At first, the taxi driver wouldn't let him in the cab. Eventually, Harry had to settle for sitting in the back with his right leg hanging out of the window all the way back to Amsterdam. He never wore that suit again."

Harry liked to enjoy himself off stage, particularly when it meant playing the piano at parties. People tended to listen to him rather than sing with him, partly because he was very good and partly because of the type of music he played. He used to play classy cocktail music like Manhattan, while Geoff Richardson's speciality was more Singalongamax. Geoff recalls an evening in Doncaster: "Harry had been playing beautifully for an hour when he had to go to the loo. So he said to me: 'Take over for a bit.' By the time he came back, the entire room was singing. He went over to Jean and said: 'I don't know, I flog myself to death for an hour, go to the loo and that little ginger-haired bugger gets on and has them singing in two minutes.'"

In some respects Harry's character was not dissimilar to that of Sooty. He was frequently up to mischief but no matter what he did, he had the uncanny knack of being able to get away with it. Jean Richardson says: "He was a very easy-going man and a real charmer, yet he also had some irritating little habits. But it was impossible to become annoyed with him for long. I remember once he'd done something that really infuriated me and I marched over to him and said: 'Harry Corbett, you're a. . . ' And before I could finish, he looked at me in that disarming way of his and replied calmly: 'Yes, I know I am.' What could you do with someone like that?"

A showbusiness friend of Harry's was little Lancashire comedian Jimmy Clitheroe, star of the hit radio show *The Clitheroe Kid*. "We went to a party at Jimmy's house in Blackpool," says Geoff, "and because he had no piano, Jimmy had arranged to borrow one from a few doors away. We somehow hauled this piano back to his house followed by Jimmy himself who, for obvious reasons, was only carrying the castors. He staggered into the lounge and gasped: 'I don't know about you lot but I'm buggered. . . '

"Harry and I had some wonderful times together," adds Geoff. "We met a lot of showbiz people and found that the ones we got on best with were the down-to-earth ones like Al Read and Mike and Bernie Winters. We went to see Mike and Bernie at Great Yarmouth once and also on the bill was an up-and-coming comedian named Jimmy Tarbuck who had just landed the job of compering *Sunday Night at the London Palladium*. He was really honoured at being introduced to Harry Corbett. It just shows the esteem in which Harry was held in those days."

Another pal of Harry's was singer David Whitfield, just about the top British recording star of the Fifties. He couldn't understand why on one stage appearance the audience was laughing at him — he thought his flies must have been undone. Then he turned round to see that Harry was mischievously leading a chain gang across the back of the stage.

When the Corbetts were playing a theatre near Sheffield, a frequent visitor to their caravan was a young impressionist just starting out on his career, Mike Yarwood. "He often popped in for a chat," said Harry, "and even then, he reckoned he'd make it to the very top. He used to impersonate me, but to be honest I wasn't particularly impressed. I'd heard him do others far better. Alan Braden, who was the musical director at Thames, later told me about all the problems he had with Mike's singing when he had his own show. Because let's face it, Mike is a wonderful mimic but by no means the world's greatest singer. Unbeknown to him, Alan used a special machine in an attempt to improve Mike's voice. Mike would listen to the playback, which was relatively tuneful, and think it was really just his natural voice. Little did he know that he had been electronically doctored."

Apart from the hectic touring schedule, Harry was as busy as ever with television, making a series of guest appearances on *The David Nixon Show* and even a coveted cameo spot with Morecambe and Wise. "Eric was dressed in a giant Sooty outfit," recalled Harry, " and Ernie was supposed to have his hand up him. Then they introduced the real thing and I came on with Sooty. I was only on for a moment, but it was good exposure. I'd met the boys some years earlier, before they had their own show, when they came up to the Bradford Alhambra. Because it was such a friendly theatre and we only lived a few miles away, we used to invite people who were appearing there out for a meal. I remember we took Eric and Ernie to Harry Ramsden's. Eric then stayed the night at our house and we had the usual party and sing-song around the piano. Eric was very quiet, apart from half-hour or so on the drums, and went up to bed much earlier than the rest of us. I think we'd worn him out."

Leslie Corbett is less charitable about that evening. "I'm afraid Eric Morecambe was an absolute misery on that occasion. He would NOT join in. He just sat in the other room playing records." Leslie's wife Muriel was even more appalled at the behaviour of singer Dickie Valentine at one of Harry's parties. "He turned up with a pornographic tape recording," she said. "I was the first to walk out of the room in disgust and one by one everyone else followed, leaving him there alone listening to his own tape. He seemed fascinated by it but I thought it was an awful thing to do, particularly when you've been invited to somebody else's home."

Although most of Harry's guest appearances on television were a resounding success, one that didn't work out to his satisfaction was *The Ken Dodd Show*. "It was a bit of a disaster. Ken wouldn't have my usual eight-and-a-half minute routine, he said he only wanted five. He cut me to make way for himself. I wasn't very pleased about it — I consider his show to have been my only flop."

Filming for television is invariably eventful, particularly when animals are involved. After all, how are they to know that Sooty is just a piece of orange cloth? He could easily be something to eat or mate with. Harry said: "For a programme called *Sooty on Safari* we went to Chester Zoo and did some filming on gibbon island. The zoo keeper warned me: 'Be careful or the gibbon will grab Sooty and you try getting him back!' We'd just started and sure enough, this animal leapt out of a tree and tried to snatch Sooty. 'Take your hand out,' shouted the keeper. 'If you don't let go you'll be in trouble.' So I had to remove my hand and allow the gibbon to take Sooty away. It dragged Sooty back up the tree, turned him over, probably to see what sex he was, but then after a minute or so, it became disappointed with the lack of response from its booty and realising Sooty was lifeless, unceremoniously dropped him to the ground. I thought: 'That's no way to treat a TV star.'

"Also at Chester Zoo, some photographers wanted me to pose for a shot with Sooty near the mouth of a hippopotamus. These people do have some wonderful ideas! They kept telling me to move back a little further so I was getting right inside this hippo's mouth. I was virtually touching its tonsils.

"'That's great. Now look at the camera,' they called.

"Somewhat agitated, I asked: 'What happens if it closes its mouth?'

"'Don't worry. We'll shout out. . .'"

The things Harry did for Sooty. Again he risked life and limb when he played the Wild Man of Zambezi, captured by those intrepid hunters Sooty and Sweep. "The last shot of that particular programme was of me dressed in a lion skin with a ring through my nose standing in a cage pressed up against the bars yelling: 'Let me out of here.' What the viewers didn't know was that the cage normally housed a killer leopard — and it was staring at me just five feet away. Before I got in the cage, I was cheerfully informed that the leopard had killed a native bearer while it was being captured. The keeper reckoned it was the worst animal they'd ever had, but I was told I'd be perfectly safe because the leopard was being partitioned off in a sleeping compound adjacent to the cage. But they didn't tell me that the gate to the compound didn't close properly, allowing the leopard to poke its snout through the gap at the bottom. All the time I was doing the scene, I could see this green beady eye looking at me. I kept thinking if it breaks through, can I escape in time? My mind was racing. I tell you, I was really glad to get out of that cage."

Another experience that Harry would rather forget occurred in the porcupine pit at Chester Zoo. It seems that the poor old porcupine isn't the most hygienic of creatures. "The stink was atrocious," said Harry, " I could hardly breathe in there. I had to take a deep breath, dive inside and wait for the call for 'action'. Our producer Trevor Hill was a very meticulous man, everything had to be just right before he started filming. I seemed to be suffering in there for ages until I heard him say: 'Where's Harry?' He'd forgotten all about me. By the time I got out, I was green!"

Sooty filming once nearly caused a full scale alert when an over-zealous coastguard at Fleetwood, Lancashire, looked through his binoculars and spotted a large crowd gathered on the beach near the boating lake. Thinking it was an accident, he contacted the police but when the boys in blue arrived, they found it was nothing more than a crowd watching the filming. And the only person who needed rescuing was Harry from Sooty's latest prank.

By 1968, Sooty had spent sixteen happy years at the Beeb, the only altercation being the Soo affair. In the early days, Sooty personified everything that the nation respected about the BBC — he was clean, trustworthy and was suitable for the entire family to watch. But the world and the BBC had changed. The year 1968 saw the assassinations of Bobby Kennedy and Martin Luther King, the Russian invasion of Czechoslovakia, the start of the present troubles in Northern Ireland and the premiere of the nude musical *Hair*. And throughout the Sixties, under the Director-Generalship of Hugh Greene, the BBC had tried to rid itself of the old "Auntie" image with brave new productions such as *That Was The Week That Was, Z Cars, Till Death Us Do Part* and controversial plays like *Up the Junction* and *Cathy Come Home*. The question was: Did Sooty and Harry still have a part to play in the future of the BBC?

CHAPTER FOUR

BUST-UP AT THE BBC

The answer was delivered by Trevor Hill just as Harry was about to take the stage for the Christmas show at the Mayfair Theatre in January, 1968. "He said: 'I've got some very, very bad news, Harry. I thought I'd tell you in person, we've got a new controller and he wants a complete change. There's no more Sooty.' I was absolutely speechless. I could not believe it. I was ready to go on stage because the show was just starting. I don't know how long I had to compose myself but you have to take a few deep breaths and get on and do it. The audience had paid good money so I had to put on a brave face and go out and say: 'Hello, lovely to see you', all that sort of thing. But inside, I was absolutely shattered. It was the lowest ebb of all time.

"It was so totally unexpected — I thought I was rock solid with the BBC. We were at the top of the tree, getting high viewing figures, everything in the garden was lovely. I didn't even know they'd got a new boss man but this Paul Fox had apparently taken over as Controller of BBC 1 and had decided to stamp his own personal ideas on everything. So he got out the broom and had a clear-out of some of the long-running programmes like Pinky and Perky and Sooty. So after sixteen years with the BBC, I was told: 'You're out'

"I thought: 'Well, that's it, we've had a good few years but that's the end of Sooty on television.' I couldn't for the life of me see ITV taking the show over after all those years with the BBC when it's a sort of cast-off glove. I had visions of Sooty and I ending up doing the beaches like Punch and Judy."

In fact the BBC didn't only think Sooty was over the hill — they thought Harry at fifty was past his prime too. Harry's agent Vincent Shaw confirms: "The BBC definitely thought Harry was too old. They wanted him to wear a wig, which he was completely and utterly against, then they wanted him to dye his hair. They also decided that, for overseas sales purposes, his northern accent was too restrictive."

The decision to drop Sooty prompted a huge outcry from children and parents alike who had grown up with him. He was a figure of reassurance to the nation, rather like Robert Dougall or Cliff Michelmore. You knew that as long as those three were on television, nothing too dreadful could happen to Britain. Now the prospect of life without Sooty was unthinkable. It would be like watching Morecambe without Wise or listening to Cilla Black without earplugs. Campaigns were started to save Sooty and several thousand signed a petition telling the BBC that they couldn't do this to him. National newspapers carried pictures of Sooty in tears.

But the despair was mercifully short-lived because Vincent Shaw had been doing his homework. As soon as he heard the fateful news, he got in touch with all the small ITV companies to ask whether they wanted to show Sooty. They all said yes. Then he approached the newly-formed Thames Television about actually making the programmes. They said they'd love to, providing the shows could be networked throughout the country. Since Shaw had already sounded out the likes of Southern, Anglia and Tyne-Tees, he was able to offer that assurance and within three days of being axed by the BBC, Harry and Sooty signed for Thames.

"What's more," said Harry, "the contract

with Thames was ten times better than the one I'd had at the BBC. The shows were twenty-five minutes instead of ten which gave me room for two seven-minute sketches, we had an eight-piece orchestra conducted by Alan Braden and we had guest stars. Ironically after the Thames signing, we were interviewed by David Frost on the BBC. It was a huge success, Frost was very sympathetic, and we then went straight back to a champagne party that Vincent Shaw had thrown. It was a great moment after the depression of thinking we were going nowhere, that it was all finished."

So did Harry feel any bitterness towards the BBC? "No, I had nothing but good feelings for them because we had sixteen wonderful years there. However, I could have killed Paul Fox — I don't think he knew anything about puppets or children's television. But I proved that Sooty was too big to die."

Before starting with Thames, Harry did take one precaution, however. Stung by the BBC's remarks about him looking too old, he went for a face-lift and had some of the puffiness taken out of his eyes. It was probably the only moment of vanity from a man who had absolutely no pretensions of stardom. Even then, it was done for Sooty's benefit rather than his own because if Harry couldn't continue, neither could Sooty. At that stage, he would never have dreamed of allowing anyone else to operate his beloved little bear.

Whilst the move to Thames was a tremendous relief to Harry, it brought despair to his brother Leslie. All the time the shows had been made in Manchester, Leslie had been able to take time off from his job with the Electricity Board in Bradford to operate Sweep but the switch to Teddington meant that he was no longer able to do so.

"I did two series with Harry for ITV," says Leslie, "but it really was hard work. Whereas with the BBC we had been recording one show a fortnight, with Thames it was twenty-six in two weeks. It was murder. I was also a sort of stage manager for Harry and therefore had to dismantle the sets. I found I was working until nine or ten every night and this was on top of working all the hours God sent with the Electricity Board. Those two weeks had to come out of my holiday and at that time I only got four weeks in all. I decided that it wasn't fair to my family to take half of my holidays to do Sweep. Muriel and I talked it over. It was a question of either giving up my job and moving down to the Dorset area where Harry had moved to or staying in Yorkshire and giving up Sweep. In the end, it boiled down to our four children. They were all getting on well at school and we didn't want to uproot them and risk harming their education. So it was goodbye Sweep — but my God it was a difficult decision.

"I had become very attached to Sweep and losing him didn't do me any good at all. He was very dear to me and to have him suddenly taken away was a tremendous blow. It got so bad that for quite a while I had to be treated for depression.

"The sad thing was not only letting go but seeing it carrying on without me and changing so much. I used to watch and look for things being done differently. I know everyone has their own ideas about a character but in all honesty the Sweep I knew doesn't exist any more."

"The parting really broke Les's heart," said Harry. "He was very upset — it made him quite ill. He loved Sweep so much. After all, he had brought him up for over ten years and he treated him like one of his own kids. The thought of someone else taking over was almost more than he could bear. He became very low and very depressed. When I visited him shortly afterwards, he said: 'Harry, you don't know how it feels. It's like losing your first-born.'

"We had ten wonderful years together but losing Sweep really knocked him for six. He tried to wipe Sooty out of his mind completely, it was too upsetting for him. In fact after a while he stopped watching the show altogether — he just couldn't bear to see someone else operating Sweep."

"We were very sorry when Les had to stop," adds Marjorie. "He was marvellous with Sweep and so quick-thinking."

Harry loved working alongside his brother not only because they both enjoyed it so much but also because it furthered his desire to keep Sooty a family business. And he had wanted to get Leslie even more involved. "After Les had been doing Sweep for a couple of years, we were in a bar one night discussing scripts and I said it wouldn't be a bad idea if we pooled our resources and got together as a proper partnership. He said he'd think about it. A week later I said:

"'Have you thought any more about coming in with me?'

"'Yes I have, Harry. I'll have a go. But you'll have to guarantee me £3,000 a year plus a percentage.'

"I said: 'Forget it. No way.'

"£3,000 was far more than he was getting with the Electricity Board then and although he had four kids and needed the security, I had two of my own.

"I said: 'I thought we were going into this as brothers. I've got to take a chance on it, so have you.' But Les was adamant about the money so the deal was off."

"The trouble was," says Leslie, "that in the old BBC days, Sooty was never really big enough to support us both. It is now because ITV pay a lot more. Maybe I do regret not going in with Harry full-time but on the other hand I often wondered where I would have progressed to in my job with the Electricity Board if I hadn't helped on the show because over the years I had to pass over a couple of chances of promotion. The whole business was a terrible wrench, made all the worse by the fact that Harry and Marjorie had moved down to Dorset in 1966. That really broke the connection since we had always been very close as a family."

Leslie's role with Sweep was taken over by another member of the Corbett clan, Harry's younger son Peter (or as he was known by then, Matthew). Peter was born in the same year as Sooty, 1948, a definite omen in view of their future association. "I was always aware that my father was a bit different from other parents," he says, "and that for some reason people seemed to take a great interest in him. I remember at primary school we were doing a project making model houses for Hansel and Gretel and because my father employed Bill Garrett, he arranged to have a model made. The whole school formed a crocodile along the pavement to walk the half mile to our house. I was most important because everyone was going to my house to see the model that my father was going to donate to this puppet play. I was also aware that the other children seemed very excited about coming to our house, so that made him seem special in my eyes.

"As the whole Sooty thing grew, it became more than my life was worth to hit Sooty or chuck him in a corner. That bear was almost as much a relative as my brother David. Older children started taking the mickey out of me and inevitably I was nicknamed 'Sooty'. Some teachers at boarding school, particularly those with a feel for Latin, used to call me 'Sooty Secundus' because my brother had been there before me.

"One of the things I particularly recall when I was young was the wild parties my parents used to have. There was a lot of smoking and drinking with my father playing the piano and my mother, who had bags of energy in those days, being very jolly and funny. She used to sing and dance and make everyone laugh. In fact, she was much more immediately funny than my father — he was basically an electrical engineer while she was a big show-off. And she loved it. Everybody from the pub used to pour back to our house and from my room upstairs, I could hear this mad noise and people keeping rhythm with beer cans. I don't know how some of them got home afterwards — in fact some didn't. I'd find them still lying around in the morning. I remember at one really noisy party sitting on the stairs with Jimmy Clitheroe. I was eight or nine at the time so we were approximately the same size. He was very unhappy about the whole thing because when men got drunk, they would try and pick him up for a joke or women would say: 'Aah, come and sit on my knee.' He hated that because he wasn't a child, he was an adult. Those parties disturbed me too because I didn't like the way that people spoke strangely when they were drunk. As a result I steered clear of drink until I was about twenty-five. Nonetheless, it was wrong for me to resent the parties. My parents had every right to throw them — and nowadays I'd love to be invited to any like them.

"When I was about thirteen and anyone was chatting to my father, they would automatically ask me whether I was going to be the person who would one day take over Sooty. I was adamant that I would not be. I didn't want to do it — I was frightened people would say: 'I know why you're doing that, it's because your dad gave it to you.' I wanted to do something on my own. My mother had always said that I would either end up on stage or in prison and teachers either liked me a lot or they really loathed me. When I was at primary school, I had played a scarecrow in a school play and people had actually said I was good at it. This was a rare experience for me because I wasn't good at much else. The one thing I was good at, but nobody ever commented about it in a nice way, was being the class fool. Later my parents decided that I should take elocution lessons from a handsome lady called Mrs. Martyn who also put on the end-of-term school plays. One year we were doing Becket and nobody was sure that I could handle it because it was a fairly heavy production and I had a reputation for being scatty. But we were sent to Leeds to watch Peter O'Toole in the film and I can honestly say it was the most moving thing I had ever seen. When we

THE SECRET LIFE OF SOOTY

performed the play, I was again told how good I was so I thought, 'I know what I'll do, I'll become an actor.' I didn't have too many alternative prospects since I wasn't doing very well academically so I applied to join the Central School of Speech and Drama. Once I'd got in, I didn't go back to school to re-sit my O Levels. I said to my parents: 'Look, I've actually done something right for once, I've got a place at drama school and it's costing you money to keep me at boarding school, I don't need to go back there.' And eventually they agreed."

When he was little, Peter felt that his father was different from other parents in a good sense, but as a teenager he began to experience the negative side of Harry's unusual occupation. "At that age, I found it rather embarrassing to think of my father earning his living with childish puppets. I thought why on earth couldn't he have been something straightforward like an accountant? In truth, deep down I was immensely proud of him, but you tend to knock it to friends. I knew when I met somebody for the first time that sooner or later they would find out what my father did. So I used to say: 'Look, before we go any further, yes, my father's the guy who does Sooty so can we get all the jokes over with now?' You know, the Steptoe jokes and holding two fingers up and saying: 'What's this? — Sooty in the nude.' Ha, ha.

"Before going to drama school, I worked on a building site for a while. This was the time of long hair, bell bottom trousers and no shoes. I had a push bike then so I was the one who got sent for the bacon sandwiches. One memorable excursion was to fetch fifteen bacon sandwiches, some cigarettes and a box of matches. I was cycling back from the cafe with everything in carrier bags when a wheel spoke went through one of the bags and ignited the matches. This in turn set the bacon fat on fire. I think I must be the only person ever to have had a push bike burst into flames! It simply burned out in the middle of the street. It was all very embarrassing — the police were called in to investigate, the traffic ground to a halt and needless to say, the guys on the building site were furious because their breakfast had been reduced to a pile of cinders."

In true family tradition, Peter was no mean musician. Back in the Sixties he had appeared on a BBC programme *The 625 Show* as part of a group called The Corbetts. The line-up was Harry (disguised with a moustache) on piano, Leslie on saxophone, David on guitar and Peter ("very badly") on drums. He went on to develop a passion for the bass guitar After working on the building site by day he used to wash the cement out of his hair, don a dinner jacket and play at local Yorkshire venues in the evenings. "Often I didn't finish until 2 am and I had to be up at 6 am to work on the building site. This was why I could often be found fast asleep on a pile of bricks in a room I was supposed to be clearing up. I got into a fair bit of trouble over that but all I knew was that I'd got two jobs, I seemed to be earning a fortune and I was having a wonderful time."

Peter was at drama school for three years but he nearly didn't make it beyond the first year. "I remember George Hall, the guy in charge, telling me: 'You shouldn't really be coming back here — if you do, it will be by the skin of your teeth. You've got plenty of talent but I don't know if I can handle what you are bringing to this college.' The problem was I was seventeen, released in London and I had this amazingly high energy level. I had never had the chance to grow up, I was really still a schoolboy when I went to college and I derived too much pleasure from being naughty. Basically, I was very immature. I knew there was another Peter Corbett with Equity and that therefore I'd have to change my name. George Hall advised: 'Don't alter it to Rick or Zap, make it something nice and long and slow. It might help you to calm down.' So I chose Matthew and became Matthew Corbett to everyone except my family, who still call me

Peter. I got up to all sorts of things in those days with high-speed living and crazy parties. I was lucky that I didn't fall into the same traps as some of my fellow students. One was killed in a car crash and another died from drugs. And my flat-mate was sent down from college after being convicted of possessing drugs. I wasn't involved but it was me who tried to bail him out in court. . . until the judge dismissed me because I was only nineteen and you had to be twenty-one to stand bail. I'm glad to say that's been my only brush with the law. Considering what was going on around me, it's amazing really that I'm still alive. Fortunately my parents were very good about it all. They simply said: 'Be careful and we won't ask too many questions.'

"One of the more innocuous things I did was never to wear shoes at drama school because in the late Sixties, that was considered to be the 'in' thing. It was pretty damn tough in winter but you didn't let on because you weren't supposed to feel pain as you had love, peace and brown rice."

On leaving drama school Matthew found that like most young actors unleashed on the outside world, the offers to become the next Olivier didn't immediately pour in. And while you may dream of the Royal Shakespeare Company, the chances are you're just as likely to end up with the London Brick Company. Matthew had a variety of jobs — he sold encyclopaedias, cleaned a disgustingly filthy block of flats and drove a taxi. None of it was glamorous but it helped make ends meet.

"I decided that I really wanted to be a musician rather than an actor so I formed a band with my brother David and a neighbour, Tony Popplewell. We christened ourselves Corbett, Corbett and Popplewell." Matthew can't remember how they came to choose the name!

"I was a fan of a group called The Peddlers and had become friendly with one of them, so we based ourselves loosely on their up-market style of music. We tried to offer the punters something other than Tom Jones, who was all the rage at the time, or "Tie a Yellow Ribbon". Like most groups, we had some terrible pictures taken for publicity purposes and started doing the pubs and clubs. One place I'll never forget was a Working Men's Club in the north-east where we were paid off after the second of our three sets. The concert chairman came over to us and said: 'I've had a word with the committee. You're bloody rubbish, get out. Here's £20.' I was devastated — I just sat in the car park and wept. It hurt like hell to be told after all our hard work that we were rubbish. But the blow was softened somewhat when we learned that what had happened to us was not an uncommon occurrence. After all, the audience didn't mind us not carrying on — they'd had two-thirds of an evening's entertainment and after six pints of Newcastle Brown, they were quite content to have a good old sing-song for the rest of the night. And what used to happen to the outstanding money owed to the band? Apparently, in many cases it ended up in the chairman's back pocket. We were told that a lot of club chairmen put a lot of pound notes in their own pockets by taking part of an act and then paying it off. Subsequently, I have heard about many highly successful, highly talented entertainers who were paid off in the same way. But at the time, I was distraught.

"Musically, we were quite good but we did have one major problem — we didn't exactly possess a terrific image. I was the front-man, David was on organ with Tony on drums. I was a born show-off like my mother but Dave is very introverted and hard though he tried, he spent most of the time looking down. He wasn't a natural performer. And Tony was even worse. His eyes would never come up from the floor. People used to say to us: 'You're supposed to be a threesome but there's only one of you looking up!' So after nine months Corbett, Corbett and Popplewell decided to call it a day and by that time anyway David wanted to train to become a teacher."

At the age of twenty Matthew reverted to acting. He rang his agent Vincent Shaw, whom he had inherited from his father, to tell him that the musical career hadn't worked out and Shaw promptly dispatched him to Bristol Old Vic where he earned £11.50 a week as an assistant stage manager, in company with Tim Pigott-Smith (who went on to achieve critical acclaim as the evil policeman Merrick in that Eighties blockbuster *The Jewel in the Crown*) and Gareth Hunt.

While at drama school, Matthew had occasionally helped Harry with the show and following his stint at Bristol, he spent a year touring the provinces with his parents, Sooty, Sweep, Soo, the whole ensemble. What had happened to the teenager who vowed never to have anything to do with Sooty? Why the change of heart? "Basically it was because I was asked by my father to help out which is very different from having to take over. Also, he was paying me and since I'd just got married to Sallie in 1969, money was all-important. For Sallie and I the tour was tantamount to a travelling honeymoon. We spent a happy year on tour and my father said that if I had any ideas for scripts, I should present them to him. So I started writing some of the scripts for Sooty and with my uncle Leslie unable to continue with Sweep for the television series, I was asked to take over that too."

Simultaneously, Matthew had begun to develop a career as a children's entertainer, on his own admission mostly copying routines that he'd seen other people do. "I had a thing called a Happy Bag and every time I tipped this bag up, the audience had to laugh. It seemed like a good idea at the time and anyway the children loved it and always laughed on cue. I also played the guitar and sang the usual array of jolly songs. In those days, every young man was expected to have a guitar and sing "Yellow Submarine" — in fact, some still do it. I had a spell doing repertory in Dundee during which time we rented out our flat in Highgate, North London, for £25 a week which was more than I was being paid in rep. So the flat was worth more to Sallie and I than my job.

"In the same repertory company at Dundee was a very talented, very funny lady who incidentally could also swear when she wanted but who is now terribly grand and a big star — Jill Gascoine. Her boyfriend at the time was Geoffrey Hayes, who to us humble performers in provincial rep. was a famous actor because he'd been on TV as DC Scatliff in *Z Cars*. Geoffrey came up and did a play with Jill in Dundee and he also did pantomime, something he'd never done before. He hated it beyond belief — he couldn't bear the thought of having to stand there and do silly things. For some reason, he didn't like me and matters came to a head when I had to fly back to London to help my father with *Sooty's Christmas Special*. In the early Seventies, flying was not an everyday form of transport and I felt really important but I think Geoffrey resented me for it. He thought he was the star, I was just a mere junior actor — flying was far too noble for me. We had a terrible row about my going off to do Sooty and he ended up saying: 'That's not what acting's about. I just cannot believe how anybody can sell their soul and work with puppets and do such stupid things.' He was really vitriolic and we nearly came to blows, it was ever so close.

"When two years later I got a job on Thames' new children's series *Rainbow*, I walked into the studio and who should I find but Geoffrey Hayes as the show's presenter! Our eyes met. I knew that he knew that I remembered what had happened in Dundee and there he was standing with George, Zippy and Bungle, knowing that nobody else in the studio was aware of what he had said about it being a ridiculous way to earn a living. Nothing was said at the time and, although Geoffrey's been presenting *Rainbow* for the past seventeen years or so, it's been an understanding ever since that whenever we meet, we don't mention it. I must emphasise though that we get along fine now."

Matthew appeared on *Rainbow* for two years, his role being one-third of the singing trio Rod, Jane and Matthew. "Rod and Jane were married at the time and I auditioned separately from them. It was Thames who turned us into a trio. They said to me: 'She looks like an angel, he sings and plays beautifully and you've got lots of character.' So away we went. When I left, my place was taken by Freddy Marks who, co-incidentally, had been my best mate at Dundee rep. What's more, he's now married to Jane! It's all very confusing."

Meanwhile Harry Corbett was not only delighted to have his son working with him, he was thrilled at the way the series with Thames were working out. "Matthew was brilliant with Sweep," said Harry. "I was so lucky that he was able to take over from Leslie without the viewers noticing any difference because Les was a tough act to follow. But Matthew had a ball and he loved every minute of it because he hadn't got the responsibility of being in charge then."

Those years with Thames were a monumental success, something beyond Harry's wildest dreams after being dropped so abruptly by the BBC. Vincent Shaw believes that the move to Thames saw *The Sooty Show* became a professional outfit rather than semi-professional as it had been before. And although Harry was, in the nicest sense of the word, basically still an amateur, he revelled in the extra care and attention he received. The first series was filmed at the Mayfair Theatre, ironically the venue where Harry had received the news of the BBC axe. "It was an outside broadcast," said Harry, "which meant that there were all these vans and people at the Mayfair for the whole week. I used to walk around in the morning, learning my lines and biting my fingernails looking at all these millions of wires going over the top of the Mayfair and thinking: 'Christ, this is all for me and a little teddy bear.'"

As Leslie Corbett testifies, it was a

demanding schedule with Thames. Harry remembered making a five-and-a-half-week series at Camberley, Surrey. "Halfway through, Thames told our producer Daphne Shadwell that she must take a break for a few days. They said that over five weeks was far too long for her to be working straight through. They weren't bothered about me though, and I was getting on for sixty! I had to be there at seven every morning, working the whole thing out. I was expected to keep going. . ."

One of the most ingenious segments of the programme was the Sooty Braden Show Band where Sooty, Sweep and Soo performed to the strains of a real eight-piece orchestra conducted by Alan Braden and featuring some of the country's leading musicians. "The band used to love it," said Harry , "and they couldn't get over the beautiful miniature instruments that Bill Garrett had made." There were exact replicas, perfect in every detail, of a tenor saxophone, harp, trumpets, a trombone, guitars, a clarinet and a double bass with a door at the back where Sweep kept his bone. These instruments alone were insured for £5,000.

Harry's personal favourite was Sooty's violin. "By using two false paws, one attached to the bow, the other to the violin, I could actually make Sooty stretch and appear to play professionally. And all the time his music was being provided by a concert violinist. It was wonderful. And then sitting at the piano was little Soo, for whom Marjorie made a new dress for every performance. Everybody took so much trouble on those shows."

Being backed by professional musicians was a far cry from the early days when Sooty (with a little assistance from Harry) used to play "The Teddy Bear's Picnic" live on the xylophone without any pre-recorded tapes or other technical paraphernalia.

However, Harry's musical training was used to advantage with Thames when, on one *Sooty Show*, he sat at the piano and played Lizst's "Hungarian Rhapsody

Number Two". "Even after playing the piano all those years in hotels and at parties, it was a different experience performing seriously on television. I must admit I was a bit wary at first, but in the end it went well and I was thrilled to bits." While Harry had fooled around at the piano on early Sooty shows, this was his first fee for playing properly on TV. Until then, very few people had known that he was an accomplished musician and the opportunity to display his prowess before a nationwide audience meant a great deal to him.

Whereas the BBC *Sooty Shows* had relied purely on Harry and the puppets, Thames budgeted for guest stars including such worthies as Hank Marvin, Dora Bryan, Freddie "Parrot Face" Davies, Deryck Guyler, old friends Janet Brown and Peter Butterworth as well as the man who calls himself Sooty's oldest fan, Roy Hudd.

The 1970's was very much the boom period for ITV when, with series such as *Upstairs Downstairs, Edward the Seventh* and *The Sweeney*, they proved to be more than a match for the BBC. This prosperity was reflected in the atmosphere at the various studios where the staff worked hard and played hard. Harry recalled: "One of the trainee producers with us at Thames was Dennis Kirkland, who later went on to work with Benny Hill. Dennis has a wonderfully quirky sense of humour that helped Sooty and I a great deal. And he was always full of ideas for the show. Off the set, he and Matthew had a whale of a time racing along the corridors, spraying each other with soda syphons. In fact, Dennis used to have to bring two pairs of pants in to work each day because one pair would get soaked through."

Understandably, the crew were forbidden to take any liberties with Sooty, Sweep or Soo but one practical joke has been practised over the years by producers on studio floor managers new to the show. At a tense moment, the producer will instruct the floor manager to cue Sooty for his lines. The floor manager looks blank.

"What are his lines?" bellows the producer, leaving the hapless victim to frantically rummage through the script before it dawns on him that of course Sooty never has any lines.

An important member of the Sooty back-up team since 1964 is Joyce Rumsey. She was working as a temporary secretary when she was sent to Harry's house in Guiseley. "My first impression was that it was a madhouse," admits Joyce. "When I walked in, there was a gerbil climbing up and down the dining-room curtains, a green and yellow budgerigar flying around the room and Mr. Corbett was 'having a few words' with Sooty and Sweep. I wasn't at all sure about taking the job on a permanent basis so I decided to give it a month's trial. But I'm still involved now, twenty-six years later."

For years Joyce was known as Sooty's secretary. "It was an incredible job," she says. "Harry was forever trying out new routines and often while I was feverishly typing away, a hand would appear round the door with Sooty or Sweep. It was great fun but most off-putting, particularly when Harry insisted on dicating scripts in Sweep or Soo's voices. It was amazing what he could do with those puppets — it was almost as if they were alive. And even though Sooty couldn't speak, Harry was so marvellous that you felt that Sooty was actually talking to you.

"Of course everyone adored Sooty. Each week children would call at the office to ask: 'Is Sooty in?' and I'd show them round. I also found that people would go out of their way to be helpful to Sooty. Traffic wardens in particular were very kind to me. I remember once being hopelessly lost in Manchester searching for the BBC studios and asking a traffic warden to show me the way. When I said it was for Sooty, she said, 'I shouldn't really be doing this' and promptly jumped in the car and directed me there herself.

"When Harry moved to Thames, he once

forgot Sweep's trombone which was urgently needed for the show. It had to go by train but having raced to Leeds station, I found to my horror that the car park was full. I was in grave danger of missing the train. I told the car park attendant of my plight. 'My grandchildren would never forgive me if I didn't help Sooty out,' he said and allowed my little blue Triumph Herald to park between a gleaming silver Rolls-Royce and a black Bentley in the station's executive car park!"

On another occasion Sooty was required for a photo call at London Airport. "The only way to get him down from Yorkshire in time was by Red Star," says Joyce, "so you can imagine the reaction I got when I filled in the form and under 'contents' wrote 'Sooty'. The Red Star people thought it was hilarious. 'Don't worry, we'll take good care of him,' they promised. And they did.

"I also had to buy some of Sooty's props. I used to have to visit a fair stall warehouse for tiny cups and saucers and because it was for Sooty, they let me have the tea-set free. I think my most unusual search was for a piece of artificial grass for a programme where Sooty was going camping. In the end, I got some from a funeral parlour where they let me have the material they drape around the edges of the graves. . ."

Despite the fenestration operations in the early Fifties, as Harry got older he had to wear a hearing aid. Vincent Shaw remembers one instance with Thames when Harry turned his deafness to advantage. "The head of children's programmes there was a woman who used to swear like a trouper. The three of us were in a meeting and she was saying: 'F—- this' and 'F—- that'. Harry couldn't hear too well.

"He said: 'What did you say, love?'

"And she repeated: 'F—- this' and 'F—- that'.

"'Oh really,' he replied and promptly turned his hearing aid off. I told him what the meeting was all about afterwards!" Matthew also has fond memories of those first years with Thames, particularly since from 1974 he was doing *Rainbow* and helping with Sooty at the same time, thereby virtually making the Teddington studios his second home. "My father was extremely pleased for me when I got the job on *Rainbow*," says Matthew, "but at the same time, I could tell that he was naturally worried that there would be a conflict of interests with Sooty. But somehow it never arose as Thames were very good at juggling the dates around."

Matthew's part in *The Sooty Show* expanded from merely operating Sweep behind the scenes to appearing as himself in a regular sequence entitled Matt and Gerry. His co-star was Gerry Marsden, formerly lead singer with Gerry and the Pacemakers, one of the most successful Merseybeat groups of the Sixties whose first three singles reached number one in the charts.

Matt and Gerry was a chaotic comedy routine written by Matthew within the framework of *The Sooty Show*. "I don't know whether the kids found it funny but we used to laugh a hell of a lot," says Matthew. "In acting, when you dissolve into unscripted fits of laughter which mean that you can't speak your lines, it's known as 'corpsing'. Gerry and I used to corpse a lot — quite a few of our sketches consisted mainly of corpsing. Gerry is the world's worst at making other people giggle, but he's quite good at not giggling himself. He'd set me off and you know how infectious giggling is, well the next thing my father, who was as bad as me for corpsing, would be helpless too. One day, it got so bad that tempers were becoming frayed because in a television studio, time is money. So the technicians were sent out of the studio. But I could still hear people laughing in the corridor outside and I could even hear giggling through a pair of headphones. Obviously they were laughing upstairs in the production gallery but had forgotten to turn the microphone off and I could hear it coming through the 'cans'. We did some terrible things — it only needed a camera to start shaking to get us going. We were like silly little boys."

But Matthew was soon to exact full revenge on Gerry. For one sketch, he was supposed to hit Marsden with a mallet which had a harmless polyurethane head. Unfortunately he missed and instead it was the mallet's wooden handle that crashed down on Gerry's skull. Gerry, who already had a custard pie in his face, was laid out cold. Matthew thought he'd killed him. Gerry went to hospital and had no fewer than sixteen stitches in the wound. Worst of all, he had to tell the doctor that he had been knocked out with a pick-axe handle on *The Sooty Show*!

Harry had more permanent health worries — his ulcer. Right from childhood, he had suffered more than his fair share of illness. At the age of eleven, he spent six weeks in hospital with a perforated appendix and nine years later he went in for three weeks to have a hernia operation. At the same time there was his deafness and from the mid-Fifties the dreadful ulcer. "Several times I had asked doctors to operate on the ulcer," he said, "but they seemed reluctant to do so." As so many of their summer shows were in the south of England, Harry and Marjorie had moved from Guiseley to a picturesque three hundred-year-old farmhouse in the Dorset village of Child Okeford. Finally in 1974 he managed to persuade a surgeon at nearby Dorchester to give him a gastrectomy. To Harry, it seemed that the operation would at last signal the end of his health problems. Instead it was only just the start.

CHAPTER FIVE

A CHRISTMAS TO REMEMBER

Harry and Matthew Corbett were both eagerly looking forward to Christmas, 1975. Harry would be brightening up the lives of thousands of children with the annual show at his beloved Mayfair theatre while for just about the first time in his career, Matthew felt really secure. "I'd got Christmas off," remembers Matthew. "I had just completed a series of *Rainbow* but there was a new batch of programmes starting in the New Year. There was no panic to look for work — for once, to use that actors' euphemism, I really was resting. There was a new contract coming up and I knew it. There was none of the dread of thinking: 'If I don't find some work in six weeks, I've had it.' It was a wonderful feeling, having enough money to buy the kids' Christmas presents and so we went up to Sallie's parents in Yorkshire, loaded with gifts."

It was a busy time for Harry, building up to Sooty's Christmas show as well as trying to incorporate things like Christmas shopping into his working schedule at the Mayfair. "I was booked to do two shows on the afternoon of Christmas Eve," he said, "which left the morning free. I hadn't yet bought Marjorie's present so I hopped in a taxi and went to Harrods. I was chasing up and down Harrods and when I got back to the Mayfair Hotel where we were staying, I said to Marjorie: 'I feel absolutely drained. I've never felt so tired in all my life.' Although I was right off colour, I managed to do the afternoon shows and then I changed my clothes and we went to a steak house in Berkeley Square. It was very cold that evening and on the way back to the hotel, I started to feel this terrible pain. Marjorie said to me: 'We're nearly there, love, so you'll be able to settle down in a few minutes.' She thought the pain could be pleurisy. I got back to the hotel and it still felt bad, but somehow I was able to get to sleep. Then at about half-past three in the morning I woke up and realised I was in a hell of a mess. In agony, I said to Marjorie: 'Get the doctor — quick.' So she rang downstairs and the hotel doctor dashed up and pumped me full of something or other and said: 'It's a massive heart attack.'

"I was just a mass of pain. I couldn't bear Marjorie to touch me. I remember she rested her hand on me to comfort me as we waited for the ambulance and I cried out: 'Don't touch! Don't touch!'"

The ambulance soon arrived. The driver said to Marjorie:

"We've got to get him into hospital straight away. Where do you want him to go?"

"I didn't know any hospitals in London," says Marjorie, "so I just said: 'Take him to the nearest. The nearest.' By then Harry was unconscious."

Harry was taken to the London clinic in Harley Street at four on Christmas morning. "I reckon I almost knocked down Father Christmas on my way there," he joked later. "And if I hadn't had a heart attack, I would have when I found out how much it cost to be in that clinic — £100 a day! But it was a saviour. If I hadn't got there, I don't think I'd have lasted much longer. Even in the short journey to the clinic, Marjorie said I lost two stone. I just shrivelled. Although I didn't know much about anything at the time, apparently they rushed me straight in and that saved my life. The surgeon told me afterwards: 'You were on your way, mate. You were going when you arrived here. If I hadn't caught you at that moment, you'd have been dead.' I was under very intensive care. This lovely Irish nurse watched over me and she told me later that three times she gave me up for dead when the line on the cardiograph machine flattened out. They had to give me another jab to keep me going."

At six Marjorie had telephoned her sons and told them the devastating news and Matthew's father-in-law offered to drive him down from Yorkshire to London. It was a petrifying journey, not only because they broke all land speed records but also of course because Matthew was worried sick. "When I got there, my father looked terrible," says Matthew. "He had lost so much weight. I thought he would die, we all did and myself, David and my mother were prepared for the worst. The room was full of flowers from the Mayfair management. My mother said that Vincent Shaw was coming round. It was a very emotional time — we were all extremely upset — and I said: 'If that man (Vincent) talks to me about money and the business, I'll kill him' because agents are famous for discussing money matters. All I wanted was sympathy and flowers — I didn't want to know about the business. I said: 'If he comes as a friend, that's alright. If he comes as an agent, I'll kill him.' So he walked in the room and after a moment said: 'Darlings, I must talk to you about the contract.' I was about to thump him but my mother restrained me. 'Don't do it, don't do it,' she pleaded."

Vincent Shaw called a counsel of war, as he termed it, where on Christmas Day the Corbetts aired their views about what should happen to the Mayfair season in the circumstances. Marjorie recalls telling Matthew:

"You've got to do the show tomorrow son."

"Tobes, I can't do the show — my dad's in hospital."

"That's the reason you've got to do it. Your father would be very upset if he thought it was cancelled. You've got to do it."

Matthew still wasn't keen. Then Vincent

Shaw chipped in. Matthew says: "Vincent explained that the Mayfair management were very nice people who cared deeply about my father but they would want the contract fulfilled because business is business no matter how sorry they were. He went on to say that when my father did come round and ask how the show's going (which would be the first thing he would ask), we could either lie and say 'fine' or say: 'Nobody's doing the show, the clinic's costing £100 a day and not only do you owe the Mayfair rent at £1,000 a day but they're also sueing you.' Vincent said: 'Wouldn't it be better for everybody if we could tell him, 'Don't worry, the show's going on. Everybody's happy?'"

Vincent Shaw adds: "It was only a great deal of pressure being brought to bear that made Matthew change his mind. Not to put too fine a point on it, I threatened him. I said: 'If you don't do it, you'll be letting down your family, Sooty and Harry.'" After careful consideration, Matthew had to agree that Vincent was absolutely right. "For a start, it gave us all something to do."

Matthew certainly had plenty to do. He had only ever seen the special Christmas show once and now he was suddenly expected to entertain audiences of children to the same high standard as his father who had been operating Sooty for the previous twenty-five years. What's more, Matthew had no time to learn the script for a performance on Boxing Day afternoon so he hadn't a clue about what was supposed to happen. "It was like *The Generation Game*," he admits. "I had the lines written everywhere — on the back of Sweep's head, under plates, on the curtains. I'd say things like: 'So you're leaving now are you, Sooty?' and somebody would push him back and I'd have to say: 'Oh, you're not leaving now? It's you that's leaving now, is it Soo?' My mother, who did Soo, was a tremendous help — she literally pushed me around the stage. The great thing was she had a microphone and, as Soo, could say: 'No, no, Matthew, it's not Sooty that's leaving, I'm going to leave. And if you were you, I'd look under the tablecloth' . . . and sure enough I'd find my next lines there."

"It was a real family pull-together," reflects Marjorie. "David ran lots of errands and answered all the phone calls while I talked Matthew through the show. I was in floods of tears during the performance. I had a spot where I dressed up in a polar bear costume and I remember waiting in the wings to go on with tears rolling down my face. Even when they said, 'You're on' and I put the head on, tears were still streaming down inside the costume. God knows how I did it. But I knew that if Harry came round and found the show had been cancelled, that would set him back. As long was the show was going, it would give him strength."

But there was plenty of laughter mingled with the tears. "At times like that," says Matthew, "when you start laughing, you're not sure whether you're laughing or crying. You can move from one to the other so easily. But lots of silly things went on — so silly, we simply had to laugh. It was an extremely traumatic time for us though. When I walked on stage for that first show on Boxing Day, I wanted to announce to the audience: 'Look, my father's dying.' But you can't do that, they don't want to know about that, so all the theatre says is: 'Due to circumstances beyond our control, Harry Corbett's place today will be taken by his son Matthew.' I honestly thought the audience would throw things at me, that they'd hate it because I couldn't handle a Sooty show. I'd simply never done it before. Yet with my father desperately ill in hospital, not only were we quite hysterical but to my amazement, so were the audiences — with laughter. And so incredibly, nobody complained. Not one person went to the Mayfair management or wrote an abusive letter. Instead they applauded loudly. Slowly but surely as the weeks progressed, I began to think: 'It's not bad this.'"

The gravity of Harry's illness was

concealed from the press initially. As far as the public was concerned, he had been admitted to the clinic purely for a rest. This decision was taken to avoid upsetting his young fans who might otherwise have thought that Sooty himself was at death's door.

While the show gallantly went on, Harry was fighting for his life. "Besides the heart attack itself, I had all sorts of complications," he said. "My kidneys packed up, I started haemorrhageing and had to have a blood transfusion and on top of that I had a stroke which left me unable to speak or write. When I did eventually get my senses going again, I couldn't believe it. I hadn't the strength to lift a finger. I was nearly lifeless.

"All I could do was concentrate on getting myself living again. I was determined to do it. I know it sounds ridiculous but I used to try and think I was Superman, that I could do anything — run fast, lift enormous weights, beat everybody at everything. It was all down to an attitude of mind, sheer will-power."

Just as everyone had predicted, when Harry was able to speak the first thing he asked was: "What about the show?" Even in the darkest moments, he couldn't bear to let the children down. And as a result of the unstinting efforts of his family and friends, he was able to be told that they hadn't missed a performance. This was a tremendous boost for Harry. As Marjorie had prophesied, if he had heard that the shows had been cancelled, it could have resulted in a major relapse. That is an indication of just how much *The Sooty Show* meant to Harry Corbett.

After three weeks in the clinic, Harry discharged himself. "They didn't want me to leave," he admitted.

"They said: 'You're not going home.'

"'Oh yes, I am,' I replied. 'You've done all you can — now I just want to get home and try and recover there.'"

Harry was still very frail and weak.

Marjorie says: "He couldn't even stand up. Instead he was wheeled out like a wet rag."

His brother Leslie adds: "Muriel and I didn't get to see Harry at the clinic because he was in intensive care but it was a terrible shock for us when we finally visited him down in Dorset. He was very drawn — he looked like an old man."

Harry had clearly underestimated the debilitating effect of the heart attack. "When I got home I was so weak that I couldn't even press down the piano keys. I hadn't the strength to get up to go to the bathroom for a shave. The kind Irish nurse from the clinic, who came down to Dorset to monitor my progress, used to help me to the bathroom but once there, I still couldn't manage to lift the razor up to my face. I thought to myself: 'I'm in a bloody bad way now — a bad way.' Nor could I manage the few stairs up to the bedroom so for months, I had a bed fixed up downstairs. It started with ten pillows so that I could sit up straight because I couldn't get my breath lying down and my recovery was charted by how quickly I was able to reduce the number of pillows. Whenever I took a pillow off, it meant there had been a big improvement in my condition. It was during those months that I realised I had come as close to dying as anyone can."

There was no doubt in Harry's mind as to what had caused the heart attack. "It was the accumulation of years and years of stress and overwork, dashing around the country with Sooty. It first manifested itself in the form of the ulcer then the heart attack." It was indeed ironic that the little bear that he cherished as if it were one of his own sons should indirectly have been responsible for nearly killing him.

Equally ironic was the fact that at this lowest point in his life, Harry should receive the supreme accolade. For shortly before that fateful Christmas, he had been notified that he was to be awarded the O.B.E. in the New Year's Honours List for his services to showbusiness.

"It was a great, great thrill," said Harry who was besieged by the press in his Harley Street bed when the news broke. "I should have gone to Buckingham Palace in the January to receive the O.B.E. but of course I was far too ill. It may sound peculiar but in in a way I was glad I couldn't go then because at the time the Queen was abroad so somebody else would have done the presentation. To me it wouldn't quite have been the same. So I had to wait until June by which time the Queen was back."

Always with an eye for publicity, Vincent Shaw wanted to make certain that Harry's award attracted plenty of press coverage that day. "With so many big names present from all walks of life, you always have to do something to ensure you get press attention on those occasions," says Shaw. "A couple of years earlier, Jessie Matthews, whom I represented, was also awarded the O.B.E. and we came up with a plan whereby she dropped the award and pretended to lose it. Fleet St. loved it and Jessie made front page news the following day. With Harry, I hit upon the idea of having a special miniature O.B.E. made for Sooty. It was an exact replica and was so realistic that a lot of people thought the Queen had actually given the O.B.E. to Sooty as well as Harry!" Marjorie got to work and made grey top hats, striped trousers and morning coats for Sooty and Sweep and together with their proud master, they prepared for another meeting with the Queen. But this time Sooty hadn't the strength to squirt Royalty with his water pistol.

"Even in June, six months after the heart attack, I was only just strong enough to go through with the ceremony," said Harry. "My face was still dreadfully pinched. To be honest, I looked like a corpse in a top hat. The Queen said how nice it was to see me again and that I'd been in showbusiness a long time. I said: 'Yes and I hoped to be in it a lot longer.' Then I started rambling on about Sooty having a new daddy because Matthew had done the stage shows. In the end, she more or less had to cut me off because I was still chatting away and there was a line of others waiting. So she gave me the medal, smiled and off I went."

The initial announcement that Harry Corbett had been awarded the O.B.E. caused considerable press speculation because also in that same New Year's Honours List was actor Harry H. Corbett, known to millions as Harold Steptoe from *Steptoe and Son*. Rumours abounded that nobody knew which of the two was to be honoured so the safest thing was to award both men the O.B.E. This was of course utter nonsense. It was simply pure coincidence that the pair should be nominated at the same time. . . but nonetheless it did make a good story.

It was by no means the first time that the public had been confused by the two. Harry Corbett (puppeteer) remembers receiving a phone call from Harry Corbett (actor) before the days of *Steptoe and Son*.

"He said: 'I keep getting your fan letters. Tell me, do you get mine?'

"I said: 'Yes, I do.'

"'Well,' he continued, 'I've decided to put an H in the middle of my name to avoid confusion.'" He later told people that the H stood for Hanything.

But the mix-ups didn't end there. Once when Sooty's Harry was appearing in Blackpool, he was phoned up by a man who was organising a big charity football match at Blackpool FC's Bloomfield Road ground between Blackpool and Tommy Steele's Showbiz XI.

"'It's going to be a really good match this,' promised the man. 'There'll be a crowd of thousands and I was wondering whether you'd be free to perform the kick-off.'

"'Me?' I said. 'Why me? I'm very flattered but I must say I'm surprised you've chosen me with all the big names that are in Blackpool at the moment.'

"'Well yes that's true but we really would like you to come along. You'd be a sensation. After all, it's a very popular programme your *Steptoe and Son. . .*'

"Could you imagine it? Little Sooty kicking off with one paw and in the middle of a huge football pitch! Nobody would have seen him, he'd have been dwarfed. Needless to say when the chap realised his mistake, he withdrew the offer so we never did get to kick off."

Harry's recovery from the heart attack was painfully slow and meanwhile there was the little question of what was going to happen to Sooty. Matthew says: "People started to mutter, 'What about the TV series that's being made in the summer?' None of us knew what to say about it because nobody knew what would be happening. We were in a state of limbo. One thing was definite, however — because of my commitments with *Rainbow*, I couldn't do the *Sooty Roadshow* that summer. So we employed Danny Ross, who used to be in *The Clitheroe Kid*, and he was to drive down and watch me do the show so that he could then take over the tour for a few months. On the way down, he had a heart attack and died in his car on the motorway. So here was the guy taking over from my father who'd had a heart attack and he has one on the way down. It was like a jinx."

In the end, a totally unknown actor called Peter Robert Scott took over for the summer shows. This was a massive blow to Harry's pride, to think that just anybody could step in and immediately be accepted by the children. "I ask you, any old actor doing MY Sooty," he complained. "After all those years, it was a tremendous blow to my ego to think that anybody else, let alone someone who had never held a puppet on his hand before, could do it. I just couldn't believe it. He'd been MY Sooty for twenty-five years and then somebody I'd never even met just wanders in, takes my place and nobody bats an eyelid. Matthew told me I wouldn't have liked it because it wasn't up to my standard but the fact remains that there were no complaints and the children went home happy. It just shows it's not me the children came to see but Sooty."

Once again it reminded Harry that Sooty was bigger than any human individual. The children didn't mind who was in charge as long as Sooty was there.

The problem of the new TV series remained. Matthew recalls: "My father did seem to be getting a little better so we decided the best thing was for me to front the programmes but to also have him present on screen, sitting in a chair, gently and quietly. But he was so stubborn, so determined to prove he was well that he was up and about far too soon, insisting, 'I'll be in that, I'll be in that.'"

Since Harry was too ill to travel to London, the mountain came to Mohammed and all the filming was done near his home in Dorset. "I was supposed to be resting," said Harry, "yet they had me filming in a chalk quarry and with all the dust I inhaled, it's a wonder that didn't kill me. Then they filmed me in a pair of shorts. I looked awful — my legs were so thin. They should have stopped me doing it."

Matthew counters: "Everybody told him how awful he looked but he didn't listen."

It was becoming apparent that the road ahead was going to be an exceedingly bumpy one for the Corbett family. For a start, Thames weren't happy about Harry and Matthew appearing on screen together — it was simply too confusing for the children. And Harry's doctor left him in no doubt as to his position. "Forget about work," he advised. " You can't do television again, that's for sure. It's out of the question. Take it easy and you'll live for ten maybe fifteen years. If you start working again, you won't last five."

It seemed inevitable that after so many years together, Harry and Sooty would have to go their separate ways. But for Harry, giving up Sooty was easier said than done.

CHAPTER SIX

COMING TO TERMS

The Sooty story has certainly seen some troubled times, but none more turbulent than the two years following Harry's near-fatal heart attack. Sooty was Harry's life. Although many people might think it as unlikely as forming a deep, meaningful relationship with an oven glove, Harry and Sooty were part of one another — and not just because of where he had his hand. Vincent Shaw believes that Sooty was Harry's alter ego. "I'm convinced of it," he says. "Often if we were discussing business over a meal in a restaurant, Harry would bring Sooty along too. And at a particularly important point in the proceedings, he would turn and say: 'What do you think, Sooty?' Really of course it was just Harry bouncing his own ideas off Sooty. Still it must be nice to be able to talk to a mirror which talks back to you and which only you can hear."

But now it seemed that their partnership was about to end. Not always one to listen to advice, Harry accepted what his doctor and his body told him — that he couldn't continue working. To Harry, there was only one thing worse than him not being able to appear with Sooty and that was for the little bear to disappear into oblivion. After all those years of hard work, that was too awful for Harry to contemplate. Somebody had to take over Sooty and the only logical choice was his son Matthew.

"It was a thing Matthew couldn't really say

no to," admitted Harry. "He had little choice but to take over, otherwise Sooty could have ground to a halt altogether. I used to say to Marjorie that if he hadn't I would have somehow got back on TV. She said: 'Oh no you wouldn't, I wouldn't have let you. If you had done, you'd have killed yourself.' Possibly, but she couldn't have stopped me. Nobody could. I definitely would have defied the doctors and gone on again to make sure that Sooty didn't just fade away. The hassle would have been thinking up new ideas but I could have got round that by going back and using what I'd already got and doing a few years calling it *The Best of Sooty*. I'd have done anything rather than let Sooty die."

So Matthew was faced with a certain amount of emotional blackmail when it came to deciding whether to do the very thing that as a teenager he had vowed not to — follow in his father's footsteps with Sooty. "Ultimately, it was a family decision," says Matthew. "My father was still too weak and was obviously never ever going to go on tour again so it looked as if I'd have to have a crack at doing Sooty. That in itself presented no great problem because my years of working Sweep meant that I already felt part of the Sooty television show. And from being on *Rainbow*, I knew all the stage hands, props boys and so on at Thames which made us like one big happy family."

On the other hand, Matthew had to consider his career and his family's security. If he took over Sooty, he would have to give up *Rainbow*. A promising career in his own right lay ahead of him. Was he prepared to abandon it all for the sake of the family business?

"After much discussion, I thought I'd give it a try," says Matthew, "although I never for one moment saw it stretching out in front of me until the present day. I went and saw my father, who at the time was so ill that he was downstairs in bed at Child Okeford, and said to him: 'Look, if we're going to do this, we'll have to do it properly — legally — because I'm risking a lot here. I already have a good job and I could go back to *Rainbow* and earn good money. I have a wife and (at that stage) two children and everything in my life is right.

"'What if, God forbid, one day you change your mind and get jealous and say: 'You're not doing Sooty, I am?'

"He said: 'I won't.'

"'But pop,' I persisted, 'people do.'

"You see, we were told that as a result of the heart attack, he may become a little odd, a little unreasonable, he may even get very angry on occasions. It was all down to the mental thing of how being so close to death can change people. I said to my mother: 'What if one of the odd things he does is take Sooty back?' She'd say, 'Harry, you can't' and he'd reply, 'Just you bloody watch me!' What if he'd said: 'Right, Matthew's in Bournemouth, I'll go to Poole and we'll see who people prefer?' What would have happened if he'd done that? I had to grow up — we all had to grow up. I know blood's thicker than water but you have to be very careful with the law. You have to tie things up legally. I said it must be clear what everybody means right at the outset because later families can fall out and there's unhappiness. So I said if I'm going to do it, it must be done my way. I've got to be the boss. And he agreed.

"Buying out my father was very difficult — money is always a tricky area when you're dealing with family. If you're not related, you go for the best deal possible but if you are related, your gain is your relative's loss and if you love your relative, it's a big problem. It was sheer hell. My father would gladly have given the business to me except the Inland Revenue say you can't give anything — one has to buy it. I was still a young person. I couldn't buy anything, I could only just afford to buy the groceries. How could I buy a business? So it had to be worked out with dad's accountants that he would forward me the money to repay the loan I was borrowing. The tangible things were a Land Rover, a van and all the props but in addition there was the goodwill (in other words the name and reputation of Sooty), which was worth an enormous amount, plus all of my father's script ideas."

Matthew bought his father out for £35,000 with Harry and Marjorie also taking a percentage of profits in the form of royalties.

The whole affair was extremely amicable, but it did put Vincent Shaw in an awkward position. He was unhappy about certain aspects of the takeover, feeling that Harry didn't get a particularly good deal. "But Harry, Marjorie and I agreed that if Sooty was to survive, I would have to look after Matthew, not Harry. It was all very difficult for me."

The crunch for Harry came after he had actually handed everything over. In total, there were sixteen tons of props and a huge five and a half ton van had to make three separate trips to Child Okeford to collect them all. Mercifully for Harry, he wasn't there to see what was nevertheless still one of the saddest moments in his life. But when he eventually returned home to the empty store-rooms, the enormity of what had happened suddenly hit him. Where were the beautifully-made sets, the musical instruments and of course all the puppets?

"When I realised I'd signed Sooty away for £35,000 along with my lifetime's work and Bill Garrett's life work, I was at screaming point. I was left with nothing except to take it easy. No Sooty, nothing. The first year of coming round was just a nightmare. I can't describe the mental pain. It absolutely knocked me for six. I was screaming inside. It was like someone hammering wires into my head — my mind was in an absolute turmoil. I knew I ought to let go but I couldn't.

"I thought: 'I can't live. I'd rather be dead than not doing the show. I'll die doing Sooty — that's how I want to go, not with my slippers in front of the fire.' I kept thinking of all the millions of children who must have thought Harry Corbett's just chucked it all in — just like that. But I had no choice.

"And the stronger I became, the worse it got. There was a feeling that I could do the show but I wasn't allowed to. I kept thinking: 'Have I got this right? Matthew's taken over and I'm not going to do any stage, TV or anything? No, no, I can't live.'"

To rub salt into the wound, Matthew even negotiated a far better contract with Thames than Harry had. "I simply told them I couldn't function at that rate," says Matthew. "I suppose you could attribute it to my sheer gall but anyway they paid me. Unfortunately my father was very hurt because he had been trying to negotiate a big rise for years." Whilst proud of his son for proving such a shrewd businessman, Harry was also a little baffled and dejected. He said at the time: "There's Marjorie and I struggling twenty-five years establishing it all and the lad's now getting nearly twice as much."

The situation was proving a considerable strain on the family. Marjorie had still been travelling up to Teddington to do Soo but hated having to leave poor Harry in bed while she did so. And Harry was left at home in the knowledge that his wife was still involved with Sooty and yet he wasn't. "It meant leaving Harry for far too long," says Marjorie. "I didn't like the fact that I had to be away from him and neither did he." So in the end, it was decided that it was best all round if Marjorie stopped being Soo's mummy on television.

"That first year was murder for me, it really was," said Harry. "The problem was that although the mind was willing, the body wasn't. Physically, I was still only about half-way to fitness."

But then Matthew came up with what Harry termed a "life-saver." It was a construction plan of a grandfather clock Matthew had found in a magazine.

"He said: 'Could you possibly make this,

pop, now that you've got a bit of time?'

"'A grandather clock? Me? I can't make a grandfather clock. You must be joking.'

"So he said: 'Well you can have a go.'

"So I thought about it for a while and decided to have a try. Matthew bought the mechanism for £60 and I took the plan and went over to my workshop. It was a struggle but I did actually manage to build this grandfather clock in knotted pine in time for Matthew's birthday. I was as proud as punch. I don't know whether it was something that Matthew had planned deliberately to give me something to occupy my mind but it played a big part in my recovery."

It also gave Harry the taste for work again, which inevitably meant his thoughts started returning to Sooty. For so long he had been too ill to even contemplate performing. All he could do was concentrate on getting stronger. But if he could construct a grandfather clock, he saw no reason why he couldn't get back to doing the show on a little part-time basis. The deal with Matthew meant that he didn't need to do Sooty again for financial reasons, it was just something that was in his blood. That he should attempt a comeback so soon after the heart attack was more than likely an example of the irrational behaviour that the doctors had warned might occur. At any rate, Harry's impatience built up until it reached the stage where he knew he had to do something about it.

"I couldn't cope with the situation any more," he confessed. "I thought I must do something or I'll go mad. So I went to the Broughty Ferry, a small hotel in Boscombe, near Bournemouth, run by a chap named Gordon Anstey who specialised in children's entertainment. I told him I could do a Sooty show for half an hour each week and he booked me."

The Broughty Ferry was a far cry from some of the splendid theatres Harry and Sooty had played in their heyday. They did the show in the hotel basement where there were no lights or other theatrical refinements and instead of one of Bill Garrett's elaborate sets, the whole thing was done in a little box like Punch and Judy. What must Sooty have thought? Perhaps it was as well that only Harry could hear.

"It was very amateurish," said Harry, "but to me, it was a real saviour. It got me started again. I felt so much better in myself just because I was back doing Sooty even though it was only on a small scale. Just to see the children's happy faces gave me an enormous tonic. It felt as if my life had a purpose again."

But Harry wasn't one to remain in humble surroundings for long. In the same way that in the Fifties he had progressed from children's parties in Yorkshire to become one of the best-known faces on national television, he now set about finding bigger and better venues for himself and Sooty.

"I did the hotel in Boscombe for about a year but then I decided I must have a proper show, so I built a set in my workshop at Child Okeford. I was constantly striving for something better. My mind was really starting to get going again, I was full of ideas. I thought: 'I must get back to doing this professionally' but I had agreed with Matthew that I wouldn't do theatres or television so I couldn't legitimately go to a theatre. But there are plenty of places outside theatres like village halls and arts centres so I followed that line of thinking and ended up in a little arts centre in Shepton Mallet which was virtually on my doorstep. This didn't upset Matthew because it was nowhere near him so I asked the woman who ran it whether she knew of any other centres that might take the show and she gave me a list. It was starting to build up nicely. I thought to myself: 'Here we go again. We're off.'"

Harry was becoming increasingly restless. He thought he had proved to himself that he was healthy enough to do the show and now he wanted to expand. "First, I wanted a better set so I built a new Sooty house in the workshop and then I wanted to move up from arts centres. I couldn't stand doing a cut-price version of *The Sooty Show* — I needed to do it professionally again, just like in the old days.

"I asked Matthew whether he minded if I did a few theatres.

"He said: 'You're at it again, you bugger, aren't you?'

"'I know I am,' I said. 'I must do it. I must do it. I won't touch your TV and I won't do a theatre or anything that would take one penny off your income. If I do, I'll pay you it.' I was just dying to get at it again."

Matthew was placed in an invidious position. "Legally I had the right to stop my father doing the shows but I just couldn't do it. Every time I saw him, he had another little idea. He even told me he wanted to do pantomime.

"I put my foot down: 'You can't, Pop.'

"He said: 'Don't you tell me what to do.'

"You hate to bring up your trump card which reads, 'I've got a piece of paper from my lawyers that says you can't do that,' so instead I had to try to talk him out of it.

"'Three shows on a Saturday is too much for you,' I maintained. 'You still find it difficult to catch your breath. This is going to kill you.'

"'Well,' he answered. 'That's the way I want to go.'

"He thought he was well and could do the show. But in truth he was still a sick man.

"It was all very confusing for me," continues Matthew. "I wanted everyone to know it was me doing Sooty now not my father. But if they kept seeing him pop up all over the country with Sooty, they'd become equally confused. It was a great battle because the people I wanted to inform were the parents, most of whom didn't even know that my father had stopped. They weren't watching the television at 4.15 in the afternoon to see me. When I used to arrive at parties, they would tell their children that I wasn't the real man who does Sooty. It was rather like being a fake Father Christmas."

The situation didn't help Harry either. Once when he did a special Sooty party, the children complained that he was the wrong man. The parents introduced him as "the man who does Sooty" and all the children shouted, "No, no, no, we want Matthew." As Matthew himself says: "It was very hurtful for my father to be told after doing Sooty for over twenty-five years that he was the 'wrong man'.

"Another factor that added to the confusion was that because newspapers only print bad stories like serious illnesses and don't print slow recoveries, many people thought my father had died from that heart attack. At the time a lot of interviewers would say to me: 'Sorry, but when exactly did your father die?' I used to say: 'Why don't you ring him up and ask him?'"

Harry and Matthew were set on a collision course which sooner or later was bound to end in an almighty crash. It came after Harry, who was pursuing an even faster policy of expansion than Hitler, decided to annexe Dartford.

"A London impressario called Charles Vance booked me into a theatre at Stafford," recalled Harry. "I thought: 'Bloody hell, that's a long way to go.' I phoned Matthew and told him about it, as promised.

"I said: 'I've got this offer to do a place in Stafford. Is that all right with you?'

"'I think you're mad,' he said, 'but I don't want to go up that way so if you really want to do it, I suppose I can't stop you.' So Marjorie and I did a week in Stafford.

"After that, I asked Charles Vance whether he'd got any other suitable theatres. I was just itching to get back into the full routine. However, I didn't want to go as far as Stafford again but he came back to me and said he had got me a week in Dartford. I said: 'Thanks very much.' It didn't click in my mind where Dartford was geographically but when I looked at a map and studied Matthew's itinerary, I was horrified. Matthew was doing a theatre in Bromley with plenty of dates in Surrey and here was I just a few miles up the road, bang in the middle of his territory. To make matters worse, the Dartford theatre was a large one — Barbara Windsor was appearing there in the evenings."

Harry immediately phoned Charles Vance. "We're in big trouble with Dartford," he confessed. "We'll have to cancel."

"We can't," replied Vance. "We've signed the contract."

"Oh, bloody hell. . ."

It was Harry's fault and he knew it. "When I told Matthew, he blew his top and he was right to do so. He was actually in Bromley that same week and one of his staff had spotted my booking and said: 'What's your dad doing in Dartford?'

"He was absolutely livid. 'Pop, you bugger,' he stormed, 'You're creeping in again and this time it's right in the middle of mine.'

"'I've tried to cancel the contract but we can't,' I pleaded. 'It won't happen again.'

"Eventually he calmed down. 'OK so we can't do anything about it,' he said, 'but I'm very unhappy about the whole business.'

"'So you should be. But I promise it won't happen again.'

"The last thing I wanted to do was upset Matthew but that one slipped through the net. After that I was very very careful."

Business relations between father and son were decidedly strained for a while and Harry was quick to acknowledge that the blame lay entirely with him.

Meanwhile in the middle, trying to keep the peace, was Marjorie. The friction became public knowledge when an interview with a frustrated Matthew appeared on the front page of the *News of the World*. The story catalogued the various disagreements and described Sooty as a monster who had split the family.

It was easy to sympathise with Matthew. "I had paid a lot of money for the Sooty business, money I didn't have. I was deep in debt. I chased enthusiastically around the country doing *The Sooty Show*, never turning down a booking, working like crazy. I remember breaking all records at Hull once, attracting more people in a week than my father ever had. This was three years after the hand-over and I thought: 'People have seen me, they've judged me and they've come back for more in greater numbers than ever.' I was so proud I rang my father to tell him.

"'That's great. Well done,' he said, but added that he didn't want to worry me or detract from my joy but he had received a disturbing letter from his accountants saying that I was still in debt to him because of the interest that had accumulated on the loan he had given me to buy the business. I couldn't believe I still owed him money. In all, it took me seven years to pay him back."

The last thing Matthew needed was for Harry, however unintentionally, to jeopardise the Sooty empire. From Harry's point of view, it has to be realised that Sooty was almost like a drug to him — he couldn't get by without his regular fix of doing a show. He was simply unable to give it up, regardless of the consequences.

The so-called rift between the two was nowhere near as wide as suggested in the *News of the World*. "It's perfectly true we had a heated discussion," explains Matthew, "but the row was only in the business sense. We were never driven apart, we never fell out socially. Indeed at the time that all this was going on, we still used to see each other at weekends and have Sunday lunch together. It never developed into a full-scale family feud."

With Harry promising to be on his best behaviour and not muscle in on Matthew's territory again, what ill-feeling there was quickly vanished and father and son continued to co-exist harmoniously in their separate worlds of Sooty.

CHAPTER SEVEN

AFTER THE HAND-OVER

So in 1976 Matthew Corbett had taken over the Sooty empire. It was a daunting prospect for a young man of twenty-eight, not only financially but also because his father had set such high standards over a period spanning the best part of three decades. He was a tough act to follow. Although on a slightly different level, it was rather like expecting Charles Darwin's son to come up with a new improved theory of evolution. And the fact that Harry was still very much attached to his creation and was soon desperate to become involved in it again made the transition that much more difficult.

What did make life easier for Matthew was that his three children were at precisely the right age for providing him with ideas for the show. Ben is now seventeen, Tamsin sixteen and Joe thirteen but in the late Seventies and early Eighties, they fitted perfectly into what has always been considered the Sooty target age, between about three and seven years old. "It was a huge bonus that when I was starting out on my own, my kids became the right age to inadvertently give me endless script ideas," says Matthew. "I was able to draw from my children's experiences and many of my early scripts derived directly from things that they had done around the house. You know what it's like, you find a couple of chairs, an old sheet and a pile of cushions cluttering up the lounge but what looks to you like the aftermath of a birthday party turns out to be a make-believe tent. In that respect, I was able to inject something into the show that my father hadn't been able to for years because David and I had grown up long ago. Also, I was the right age for children to relate to because whereas my father was the age of their grandfathers, I was approximately the same age as their fathers."

When Matthew bought his father out, Harry adopted the title of "Sooty's consultant". But he could see that Matthew was desperate to do the TV show his way and didn't want to be seen to be interfering. "It was a great thrill for him," said Harry, "and although the circumstances leading up to the takeover were hardly ideal, I was thrilled for him. At that stage I was too ill to even consider doing Sooty myself so my main concern was to see the show continue. When he came to do his first series, I thought it was best if Marjorie and I kept out of the way and we went on holiday down to Sidmouth. I rang Matthew to tell him but he was horrified.

"He said: 'You're not going away, are you, just when I'm starting my first series? I might need you!'

"'No you won't,' I said. 'Come on, you wanted to be the boss. But look, I'll be on the phone in Sidmouth and if you need me, I'll be up like a shot.'

"Initially Matthew was on the phone quite a bit asking for help but after I assisted him with the first thirteen, it really did become his own show. For the second year, he tried out a space series but I'm afraid it didn't work terribly well. Thames told him: 'We'll try one more series of Sooty but we want it more down to earth like your father used to do it.' So he reverted to a domestic show with a bathroom, a bedroom and a kitchen which really is where little children are happiest because that's their environment at that age."

Matthew swiftly discovered that in this country at least children's entertainers on television have to be constantly on their guard. No matter how innocent a

SOOTY LIMITED

REGISTERED OFFICE

Harry and Sooty hit the big time in the early Sixties, and the little bear became the base of a commercial venture

Sooty could have been sent to the Tower for squirting Prince Philip (hidden behind Her Majesty), but fortunately the Queen saw the funny side

Michael Aspel produces a Big Red Book and a Little Red Book to surprise Harry and Sooty on This Is Your Life in 1988

Matthew marries Sally — and look who turned up

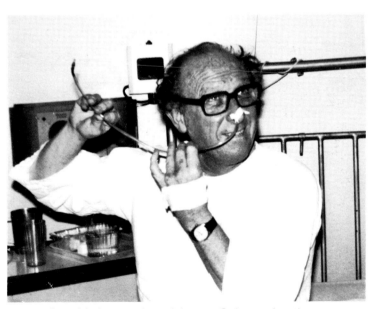

Harry does his impression of James Galway after the operation on his stomach ulcer

While recuperating from his near-fatal heart attack, Harry received the O.B.E. from the Queen at Buckingham Palace. And Sooty demonstrates what the well-dressed bear should wear on such occasions

The fateful moment when Sooty squirted Barbara Woodhouse. Furious Barbara stormed off, complaining she was drenched. Dogs are clearly easier to control than little bears with water pistols

Dog training HIS way — shortly after this picture was taken, one of the trainee police dogs tried to take a lump out of Sooty

Hello possums! A meeting of megastars, Dame Edna and Sooty

Sooty demonstrates the new secret weapon of the British Army Air Corps on Corporal Ben Barton in Hong Kong

Matthew's stage show deputy Connie Creighton prepares for lift-off

One of Sooty's greatest fans, George Harrison's son Dhani, with his dad

As Michael Parkinson will tell you, it's a brave man who tackles Rod Hull and Emu. No wonder Sooty came armed

programme is, it needs only the slightest moment of indiscretion, even flippancy, to cause an army of irate parents to reach for the telephone or the notepaper and complain to the broadcasting authorities that their children are being corrupted. As an added hazard, certain sections of our society seem to thrive on objecting to the contents of children's programmes.

Sooty has fallen foul of many groups in his time. Aside from the BBC's disgust at the arrival of Soo bringing sex to the show, he has been chastised on a number of occasions. A scene was cut from one of Sooty's road safety films after mothers in the Medway towns disapproved of Sweep putting his bare paws in a smoking oven.

Matthew was amazed when a viewer sent him a bill for a tube of toothpaste after a child had copied Sooty by squirting it all over the mirror. And following the annual festive show at the Mayfair, Matthew received a bill for £6 from a man who claimed his silk tie was ruined after Sooty had squirted him with the water pistol. So much for Christmas spirit. . .

Never to be outdone, ardent feminists jumped on the bandwagon by condemning the show for forcing Soo to do menial jobs such as tea-making, washing-up and cleaning. This, they maintained, was a typical example of men's chauvinistic attitude towards women. Matthew felt he over-reacted somewhat, because for the first programme in the next series he had Soo mending a motorbike while the boys stayed in the kitchen and made fairy cakes. Happily, sanity was soon restored and Soo went back to what she liked doing best even if it was derogatory to female pandas.

There were complaints too when the show featured a real baby lying on its back, appearing to be bottle-fed by Sweep. The punch-line was that the baby then squirted the milk back in Sweep's face. In reality of course, Sweep wasn't feeding it anything but this didn't deter an irate nurse from writing in to condemn the programme for implying that a baby could be fed on its back. "This is totally wrong," she stormed. "A baby should never be bottle-fed lying in this way." She presumably thought most mothers-to-be picked up tips from *The Sooty Show* rather than the maternity clinic. She also deplored the fact that there was no adult present at the time — only Sweep. It obviously escaped her attention that the studio was indeed full of adults, namely an entire television crew comprising cameramen, sound men, lighting men, props men, floor managers, make-up artists and wardrobe supervisors, not to mention puppeteers. For although she clearly believed Sweep to be real, he does need a helping hand from a human.

Matthew also landed in hot water over a character who appeared on Sooty's TV show called Banana Briggs, played by comedian and EastEnders star Mike Reid. Matthew says: "Banana Briggs was the archetypal cartoon burglar, complete with flat cap, Lone Ranger mask, swag bag and striped T-shirt. As his name implies, everything he did revolved around bananas. One day on the show he marched in brandishing a banana and shouted:

"'Stick 'em up.'

"'Don't be ridiculous,' I replied. 'That's a banana.'

"'Yes,' he said, 'but this banana is loaded.'

"So it was a pretty silly situation, yet a woman wrote to the Independent Broadcasting Authority to complain that not only was I glorifying burglars but that I had made her child terrified of bananas! Apparently on seeing Banana Briggs, the child had jumped behind the settee in hysterics and cried: 'That man's going to shoot Matthew with a banana.' So from then on he thought a banana was an offensive weapon. Anyway, far from saying, 'Look madam that's a really silly complaint you've got', the IBA passed the letter on to Thames accompanied by a note which said: 'This may sound trivial to you but because

Sooty is so popular, we're trying to protect him. We don't want anything to tarnish his reputation. We want to make sure that nobody can possibly criticise him.' And next morning the Head of Children's Programmes at Thames duly hauled me over the coals and warned that it must not happen again.

"I've had complaints about the stage shows too. Parents have written in to say that when the lights go down at the start and the theatre goes black, their daughter has burst into tears and they've had to leave straight away because she's afraid of the dark. If they knew that, why did they bring her in the first place? Yet they blame me. Or there'll be a stunt where a car door falls off and there's a flash and a bang. Ninety-nine point nine per cent of the audience burst out laughing but if one child cries, I get a letter accusing me of being irresponsible and of frightening children.

"But the worst one of all was on television back in 1980 and it was the nearest to a genuine national scandal there's ever been with Sooty. It was a terrible business. In the programme, Sweep was becoming hyper-excited and was rushing round all over the place so he was put in a cubicle which was called, and this is where we went wrong, a tranquilising booth. Then Sooty pushed a button on the booth, there was a lot of smoke and eventually Sweep emerged, looking decidedly dozy. The programme was a repeat which meant that five million viewers had already let it go as had another 4,999,999 this time. But one lady in Southampton objected to it and rang her local radio station. She told them that she had just watched *The Sooty Show* and had seen Sweep using tranquilisers, which was inaccurate for a start.

"So the radio station asked its listeners: 'What do you think of Sooty using tranquilisers?' And the listeners, who probably hadn't even seen the programme, said they thought it was disgraceful. The next thing was a newspaper reporter overheard the radio debate and put a story in the local press under the heading:

SOOTY AND SWEEP IN TROUBLE OVER TRANQUILISERS

"From there it just snowballed. *The Daily Mirror* picked it up, followed by *The Sun*, *The Daily Express*, LBC, Capital Radio, the lot. And they all rang Thames and, to make matters even worse, the IBA. And the story had become distorted out of all proportions. Suddenly Sooty was being accused of pushing drugs on the show — hard stuff like purple hearts and cocaine!

"It was a nightmare for me. The phone never stopped ringing. The moment I put the phone down from talking to one journalist, another was on the line. It was all very unpleasant. It's tempting to lose your temper because the whole thing had arisen out of one person being stupid but you have to keep cool. In the end, Thames decided to remove the scene altogether by which time of course it was too late.

"After that, a "Sooty Rule Book" was introduced so we knew exactly what we could and could not use on television. It just shows how careful you have to be."

Matthew is acutely aware of his tremendous responsibility. One *Sooty Show* included a bathroom scene in which there was a scrubbing brush complete with wires. "The brush wasn't connected to electricity on the programme but because of the wires, it looked electric. About half a dozen people wrote in to complain and on this occasion they were right to do so. As a result that show was re-edited before being sold to Australia.

"I'm actually very glad that the IBA does pay special attention to us and do vet the show so heavily. It not only means that I have to maintain high standards but it is also a compliment. They say that Sooty's influence with children is about as powerful as you can get —

whatever he tells them sticks in their minds. If Sooty tells kids to buy a certain brand of sweets, they'll do it. And that is the reason why we have never been allowed to advertise children's products on television because it would constitute unfair selling."

Sooty was offered commercials for Smarties and Cadbury's Wispa (an obvious choice) but the IBA turned down the idea on both occasions. The Milk Marketing Board wanted Sooty to succeed the Humphreys and their famous "watch out, watch out, there's a Humphrey about" adverts but again the IBA rejected the proposal, stating that Sooty is simply too powerful for young minds.

In showbusiness terms, Sooty changing hands from Harry to Matthew and still sustaining his tremendous popularity has been a unique achievement. It would be hard to imagine Emu carrying on regardless if Rod Hull were to suddenly find another use for his right arm. And where would Lord Charles be without Ray Alan? Or Orville without Keith Harris? Although in the last case it would be nice to speculate. But Sooty's progress was totally unaffected. Not only did viewers continue to tune into the television programmes in vast numbers but they flocked to the stage shows too. For example in 1979 Sooty's matinee at the Royal Court Theatre, Liverpool, did consistently better business than the voluptuous Fiona Richmond's *Yes We Have No Pyjamas* which was playing in the evenings. Clearly audiences preferred a little bear puppet to a little bare flesh.

Naturally the hand-over had a profound effect on Matthew's family. "My kids react to me in totally different ways," he says. My daughter Tamsin is very proud of me and of what I do. If we're out and passers-by start pointing and muttering, 'Is that him off the telly with Sooty?', Tamsin will stand beside me and link arms so that everyone knows she's part of it. She actually enjoys the recognition. My younger son Joe is so lively, such a massive bundle of energy that the whole thing completely washes over him. On the other hand, my elder boy Ben thinks of me in much the same way as I used to think of my father at that age. In other words, he is quietly proud but he also finds it all acutely embarrassing. For Ben at seventeen, the fact that I do Sooty is mortifying. It's very difficult for him to handle. He must wish: 'If only my dad was something ordinary like an accountant.' He won't let anybody know what I do even to the point of telling little white lies. People will see me on screen and say to him: 'Is that your dad on TV?' And he'll say: 'I don't know what you're talking about. No, it isn't.' He doesn't want to know. The moment I appear on television, he simply walks out of the room!

"It has been even harder for Sallie, my wife, because she had a life before Sooty. Sallie is not theatrical, she is a trained psychiatric nurse which means if I break my leg she's hopeless but if I rip all my clothes off in the middle of the street, she'd know how to deal with it. She has saved me from being more unbearable than some people think I am because she won't allow me to become too precious. The trouble with theatrical people is that many of them believe their own publicity. People come and see you doing a ninety-minute show and afterwards they say: 'You must be exhausted.' So you think: 'Yes I am tired, I'm worn out' whereas in fact you probably haven't done as much work as they have that day. As a nurse Sallie worked far harder than I do. I'd come home and sigh: 'I'm exhausted.' And Sallie would say: 'You're tired! Do you want to know what I've been doing today? I was up at six washing old ladies, changing beds and then I had a fight with a guy who had an armchair and was trying to kill me. And you say you're tired! And what's more you can earn more in one Sunday afternoon than I get in a whole month.' But an actress wife would say: 'Come and lie down, I'll call a doctor.' And that would be no good for me. So Sallie has been a tremendous help in stopping me getting carried away with my own importance.

"Sooty hasn't done Sallie very many favours. Sure he's given her things in a materialistic sense — a nice house in Camberley, Surrey, and a car — but he's also stolen her career. She worked hard as a mature student, passed her exams and rose to the position of nursing sister but it became clear that if she was a nurse and I was away on tour, we'd be ships that pass in the night. And we didn't want our marriage to go the same way as so many others in showbusiness. So about five years ago, Sallie took the brave, unselfish decision that her career would have to take a back seat and she has become Mrs. Matthew Corbett. And because this is 1990 and not the era of our parents, some days that gets straight up her nose. She has been encouraged to become an individual but now she's expected to do the housework and run around after the kids. It's fair to say we've had a few ructions about showbusiness but I love her and respect her.

"It was so much different for my mother and father because they had started Sooty together. They were a unit. Although she wasn't seen on screen, my mother was as much an integral part of the act as my father. But Sallie had no connections with Sooty until she met me. And whereas my mother revels in being known as Sooty's mum and will even offer that as a title, Sallie doesn't like being called that at all."

While accepting that when Sallie was a nurse she probably worked harder than he did, Matthew is quick to point out that being in control of the Sooty empire is a pretty tough assignment in itself. "If you think it's an easy job being in charge of Sooty, forget it. People see me on stage for ninety minutes looking relaxed and they think that's all I do each day and how simple it all must be. Or they believe that apart from the three months when they see I'm on television, I don't do anything else for the remainder of the year. They think it's one long holiday. But it's really hard work, often non-stop. Not many people realise quite how much time, effort and money goes into presenting a show such as Sooty's. A very small percentage of my life is actually spent on stage, and even though that would appear to be the glamorous bit, it often isn't. It's just my job to make it look so. An awful lot of time goes into thinking up ideas that haven't been done before and after all these years, that becomes more and more difficult. Then there's the travelling to stage shows. Because I like to try and get back home to Camberley after each performance, even a relatively short trip to somewhere like Essex for a week necessitates my spending five or six hours a day in the car in addition to doing the show itself. And when I'm not touring the country or at Thames rehearsing and recording the TV shows, there is so much organisation to do, so many people to deal with, so much work behind the scenes that the public don't know anything about. Consequently, I'm not always best pleased if anyone suggests to me that Sooty's just a part-time job and what do I do in my spare time?"

In spite of the toil, Matthew has reaped enormous rewards from Sooty — and not all financial. "One thing Sooty has given me," he continues, "is power over the most extraordinary people. When I appeared on TV-am last year, I not only got a kiss from Jerry Hall but she had to ask ME if I could give her some signed photos because her and Mick Jagger's son James is a big fan of Sooty. That little bear also meant that George Harrison, who was a hero of mine at school, had to ring me up and ask ME for a favour. It all came about because his son Dhani had said: 'Daddy, daddy, please can you get Sooty to come to my birthday party?' I agreed but insisted on doing the party for no fee because that way I was able to meet George on an equal footing — I wasn't merely an employee of his for the afternoon. As a result, we've become firm friends. We've been to dinner at each other's houses and Sallie and I actually ended up eating a Chinese meal out of tin foil wrappers in George Harrison's kitchen.

So as a direct result of the power of Sooty, I am now mixing socially with part of The Beatles. It's unbelievable.

"George also said to me once: 'By the way, Ringo wants your autograph.'

"I was dumbfounded. 'Ringo wants MY autograph?'

"'Yeah,' replied George, 'but Ringo's bloody mental anyway!'

"That certainly put me in my place."

Many years earlier, Matthew had met another pop legend who turned out to be a great fan of Sooty. "I was a young lad of about thirteen and had become interested in the guitar. One day my father took my brother David and I to meet Cliff Richard and The Shadows who were appearing in Blackpool. My father went to the stage door of the theatre and introduced himself. 'I'm Harry Corbett, I'm on at the pier. Could the boys say hello to Cliff and The Shadows?' So he knocked on the dressing-room door and Cliff was getting changed. As we stood there, Cliff said: 'Sir,' (I distinctly remember him calling my father 'sir') 'please come in and before you say a word, could I just say how much I love what you do and respect it.'"

Sooty's other musical fans include Tommy Steele, who formed a mutual admiration society with Harry and brought his daughter to the show at the Mayfair, Alvin Stardust, who actually wrote a song about Sweep, and most unlikely of all, heavy metal rock group Iron Maiden. The connection with the head-banging bikers stemmed from the son of Iron Maiden drummer Nicko McBrain who desperately wanted his daddy to be seen with Sooty. So Matthew invited Nicko on to the programme and in return Sooty now features heavily in all Iron Maiden concerts. In fact Nicko has been lowered by crane onto stage wearing a full-size Sooty costume, specially lent to him by Matthew. It's just as well it isn't bat-eating rocker Ozzy Osbourne who's a Sooty freak otherwise he would probably have

THE SECRET LIFE OF SOOTY

bitten Sooty's head off on stage! Other guests on *The Sooty Show* in the Eighties have included strong-man Geoff Capes, swimmer Duncan Goodhew, bird-man Percy Edwards, disc jockey Dave Lee Travis and Goon Spike Milligan, whose appearance gave Matthew particular pleasure. "I wrote an insane script for Milligan as an old man in a wheelchair," says Matthew, "and afterwards he said he'd had a terrific time and what's more he thought it was very funny. For me to write something that Spike Milligan thinks is funny is one of the highspots of my career."

Matthew was also elated when John Cleese came to see the show at the Mayfair. "It was very difficult for him," says Matthew, "because he's so tall and of course virtually everyone else in the audience at the Mayfair is tiny. But after the show he came backstage with Connie Booth, shook my hand and said: 'I must thank you so much. You have given myself and my family so much enjoyment.' What a wonderful gesture. I felt that I should have been thanking him for coming."

In recent years, Sooty has made guest appearances on such programmes as *Jim'll Fix It* (where Matthew was a little girl's idea of a handsome prince), *The Paul Daniels Christmas Show*, a Jim Davidson Special and in 1982 he starred in a half-hour Thames documentary to mark thirty years of his television show. To celebrate that anniversary, Sooty threw a party for the patients at Great Ormond Street Children's Hospital in London and they all tucked into a huge cake made in the shape of a television set. Of course that is the caring face of Sooty, but we all know what he is capable of in his less-disciplined moments when he adopts a James Dean-like expression and becomes *Rebel Without a Voice*. As in the days of Harry, he has squirted the famous, dousing such notable victims as Terry Wogan, Russell Harty, Jerry Hall and George Harrison (the latter with a soda syphon). Celebrities have always taken the water-pistol treatment in good spirit and so they should as it's only a little jet of water. But what didn't offend Prince Philip was deemed outrageous behaviour by the late Barbara Woodhouse, a woman who had the reputation for having endless patience with dogs but very little tolerance of her fellow human beings.

"Of the hundreds of personalities who have been squirted by Sooty," recalls Matthew, "Barbara Woodhouse was the only one who ever objected. She didn't like it at all. We were at Bradford Alhambra and we were going to see if she could train Sooty in the same way that she trained dogs on television. I had warned the clutch of photographers in advance that Sooty was going to squirt her so they could get a good picture.

"At the given moment, I said to her: 'Sooty's got a little present for you' and out came the water-pistol for a quick squirt, nothing much at all.

"But when the water landed on her, she went mad. 'Oh, oh, you foolish boy,' she raged.

"The room went silent and everybody looked at the floor. I was left standing there alone to face her wrath.

"'You wet me. I'm wet,' she continued. 'I can't believe that you've done this to me.'

"Trying to ease the situation, I pleaded: 'Don't blame me, it was Sooty.' Surely this would make her see how ridiculously she was behaving? How could anybody get that upset by a glove puppet? But she could and, distinctly unamused, she stormed out."

Sooty's water-pistol also caused chaos when he and Matthew were interviewed on BBC Radio Hull to promote the stage show in the town. As a friendly goodbye, Sooty squirted the disc jockey but unfortunately the water seeped into the faders, which are important items of radio technical equipment, and the station was forced off the air for forty-five minutes. "I don't think we were too popular at the time," reflects Matthew, "but the next occasion we went there, the station said it was the best

THE SECRET LIFE OF SOOTY

thing that had happened to them in years. Disc jockeys kept coming up to me and saying: 'Any time you want to squirt my faders, you're welcome.' It was because the whole episode had attracted plenty of television and press coverage locally and had really put the station in the spotlight. Because let's face it, it's a great story, a radio station being forced off the air by Sooty!"

Under Matthew's guidance, Sooty progressed successfully into the Eighties and Nineties. And while maintaining the old traditions (Sooty and Soo have still yet to tie the knot), the show has had to move with the times to avoid becoming another long-forgotten childhood relic like Jan and Vlasta Dalibor's Pinky and Perky. Terry Hall and Lennie the Lion are rarely seen on television these days and even that foxy old stalwart Basil Brush seems to have been ousted in the popularity stakes by the more caustic Roland Rat. Nevertheless while others have fallen by the wayside, Sooty has managed to adapt to contemporary life. Today's children enjoy seeing Sooty and his friends disco dancing just as much as millions enjoyed watching him do the jive in the Fifties while their older brothers and sisters were switched on to the new breed of pop shows like *Cool For Cats*, *Six-Five Special* and *Oh Boy*. And he still has a considerable adult following. Each week Matthew receives many letters from senior citizens and shift workers saying how much they enjoy the programme.

Vincent Shaw, who is still Sooty's agent, admits: "I think it's fair to say that when Matthew first took over, his relationship with Sooty was very bad. But he's extremely professional and he's come to terms with Sooty and year by year he's improved steadily. As far as television is concerned, he now presents the show in a much better way for today's generationthan Harry would have done. Harry was a genius with Sooty, no doubt about that, but in the nicest possible sense he was also an amateur whereas Matthew is a very accomplished professional."

Some people think Matthew's attitude is too hard-nosed and compare it unfavourably to his father's relatively easy-going approach. But the fact remains that these days you have to be tough to survive in business, you can't succeed on friendly handshakes and gentleman's agreements any longer. Without Matthew's energy and commitment, Sooty would probably not have lasted through the Eighties.

To Harry, Sooty was above all else a friend. But to Matthew he is principally a piece of merchandising. Matthew is very grateful to Sooty, but doesn't feel terribly sentimental about the puppet. "Dad was far more romantic about Sooty than me," he says. And whereas Harry would turn back if he had forgotten to take Sooty in the car on holiday, Matthew once said he would turn back if he found that he HAD got Sooty in the car on holiday! Having said that, Matthew certainly wouldn't allow Sooty to be thrown around the room. Harry was always worried in case it hurt Sooty's feelings but Matthew's reasoning is more practical — acts of physical violence can ruin the puppets and new puppets cost money. Matthew estimates that each year he gets through about a dozen Sootys for the television series and a similar number on stage. Incidentally, the stage Sooty is slightly larger than the TV version so that he can be seen from the back of theatres. In all, it means that over the years there have been in the region of a thousand Sootys.

However, Matthew is quick to point out, with his tongue firmly planted in his cheek, that there is of course only ONE Sooty. All the rest are his stand-ins, in the same way that a film star uses stunt men to remain in pristine condition. Matthew has grown so accustomed to being asked how many Sootys there have been in all that he has formulated a standard reply to avoid shattering the illusions of children and sensitive grown-ups alike. "There is some sad information to be learned about Burt Reynolds," he confides, "and it is very relevant to Sooty. That is that when you see Burt Reynolds in a film and he's driving along in his car and the car goes over the cliff, I have to tell you that it's not actually him in the car. Burt has stand-ins — he's too valuable to risk. Equally, Sooty has little stand-ins because he too does things that are dangerous and messy and he may get damaged." And I always thought the main connection between Burt Reynolds and Sooty is that Burt looks as if he's wearing Sooty on his head.

On the subject of Sooty statistics, it is estimated that there have been in the region of seven hundred TV shows since 1952. If they were run consecutively, they would occupy over a week of non-stop television. Add on the vast number of stage shows and the staggering result is that in total there have been nearly fifteen thousand performances of Sooty since time began. Even Wogan can't match that.

One of the major differences between father and son is that Matthew is much more forceful. "I think I've got a stronger presence than my father had," says Matthew. "Harry had two sons — David has all the talent and brains and I've got all the gall and push. If one son had combined all those qualities, he would have been a world-beater. David is a brilliant musician but he's so modest that he'll say he can't really play the piano when of course he can. But me, I've got the nerve to say I can sing when I can't. And I've got this relentless drive. Sometimes I wish I didn't have it, because drive makes you do things that you don't need to. For example I don't need more money but for some reason I want it."

Harry described Matthew as a "hardened businessman". It was not meant in a derogatory sense at all, merely to illustrate his son's determination to keep the Sooty empire flourishing. For not only did Matthew negotiate a considerably better pay deal from Thames, he also took significant steps to increase public awareness of Sooty through merchandising — a side of the business that he felt had been allowed to slip during Harry's latter years at the helm.

From the mid-Fifties Sooty's licensed merchandising had been looked after by Peter Barker Ltd. When Peter Barker took over, the only item on sale was the Sooty glove puppet, but steadily he expanded the range to everything from wallpaper to pyjamas. "The aim," says Barker, "was to bring out half-a-dozen products a year and just let things drift along. Harry didn't want the market flooded — that could have killed Sooty stone dead. I felt that by doing things quietly and methodically, Sooty would have a much longer life. But when Matthew Corbett took over, it was clear to me that he was a young man who wanted to go places in a hurry, much faster than we had with Harry. He and I didn't really see eye to eye — he thought Sooty was not being properly exploited and that there was room for improvement. There were a lot of people in the market at that time and I wasn't getting any younger so I thought it best to leave."

While Matthew was intent on reviving the merchandising, he too was aware of the pitfalls of characters that become crazes. "The trouble with trends," he reasons, "is that they become crazes and burn themselves out, like Cabbage Patch Dolls. I want to make sure that Sooty is here to stay."

Vincent Shaw adds: "The reason why Sooty has been such a success for so long is that we have never allowed him to become fashionable, because something that becomes fashionable soon becomes unfashionable. We have always deliberately just kept Sooty on the boil. We have never gone for the money. And as a result of that approach, Sooty has had, and is still having, a much longer life. The other thing to bear in mind, of course, is that Sooty has remained popular for all these years because he is socially acceptable. He is naughty but nice."

The other great advantage of not inundating the market is that you don't infuriate poor long-suffering parents. With Sooty, you know the only puppets to buy are

143

Sooty, Sweep and Soo, unlike toys such as the Care Bears, where no sooner has a child collected the principal characters than they all sprout add-on relatives. It is deeply annoying when a parent thinks there cannot possibly be another Care Bear to buy, only to find that Birthday Bear has suddenly acquired a second cousin twice removed. . .

One way in which the golden bear's profile was raised was by the opening of a Sooty museum at Shipley, Yorkshire, in December 1987. Called The World and Sooty Museum, it tells the story of Sooty right from Harry's humble beginnings as well as exhibiting some of Bill Garrett's finest sets (Bill himself died in 1982, aged seventy) and showing videos of the gang's more recent escapades on television. The museum was partly opened as somewhere for Matthew to store all the paraphernalia that had accumulated over the past forty years, but it has rapidly become a popular tourist attraction. In its first year it attracted twenty-one thousand visitors and in 1989 some fifty thousand came to share in the magical world of Sooty. The museum is also an ideal outlet for merchandising and a wide range of goods (glasses, beakers, jigsaws, writing pads, party packs, painting books, gloves, sweaters and of course puppets) is on sale there. It is also the home of Sooty's fan club and the base of Patsy B Marketing Ltd., the firm who now handle the merchandising side of Sooty and who took over responsibility for the making of the puppets from Chad Valley in 1980. But it grieves me to disclose that Sooty, that most British of institutions, is now actually made in Taiwan. Is nothing sacred?

So Sooty is very much an international organisation and Matthew has also taken significant steps towards achieving one of his great ambitions — to make Sooty a truly international performer. It was always Harry's great wish too, but he set his sights on the notoriously difficult American market. "The trouble with the Americans," says Matthew, "is they can't grasp the concept of a bear that doesn't talk and a dog that squeaks!"

But these days Sooty is a major star in such far-flung places as Australia, New Zealand and Hong Kong. It was one thing selling the television programmes to these countries but another matter altogether to attempt to put on stage tours. In addition to the vast amount of time and hard work involved in mounting such ventures, they presented a considerable risk financially. "I've found that there are few people with real courage in this world," says Matthew. "Vincent Shaw has courage and so does a sixty-five-year-old businessman named Arnold Fry. He is the only man who has been brave enough to take Sooty and I abroad. It's always nerve-wracking taking the show to a new country. You never quite know what to expect. When we went to Hong Kong in 1987, I was really worried as to how we would go down, but my fears were unfounded because every performance at the one thousand-seater Hong Kong Arts Centre was a sell-out. The public and press loved it. I felt so proud because we had overcome so many problems to get out there."

While in Hong Kong, Matthew and Sallie, who acted as stage manager, were given a conducted helicopter tour of the region by the British Army Air Corps 660 Squadron. The soldiers all turned out to be great Sooty fans. . . even after he'd produced his own top secret weapon, the water-pistol. There aren't too many people who could get away with squirting a highly-trained soldier with water.

Although the now-defunct *TV Mirror* magazine reported that the black and white Sooty shows sold to Australia in the 1950s were too sophisticated for the natives, the Aussies have now progressed culturally to the extent where they can appreciate and understand Sooty. "They adore him out there," says Matthew. "It's funny because the latest batch of programmes sold to Australia are still about ten years old. I've got long permed hair and I'm wearing bell-bottom trousers. They're a real culture shock. The videos are more up-to-date however, not that it really matters because the main thing is that Sooty and Sweep still look the same. But I do get some strange looks when I go out there in person. They worship Sooty and I got an enormous thrill out of telephoning my father on his seventieth birthday from a hotel in Melbourne and reading him a huge story splashed across the papers out there bearing the headline:

SOOTYMANIA SWEEPS AUSTRALIA

"It was a wonderful write-up, reporting how Harry Corbett's creation had captured Australia. I was able to announce to the audience: 'Today my dad, Harry Corbett, is seventy years old.' And all the adults stood and applauded. To think, half-way round the world an audience were applauding a man in Dorset for something he did for them when they were little. It is quite staggering. When I related all this to my father he was in tears of joy. I think it was just about the best birthday present he could have had. And it's exactly the same in Hong Kong and New Zealand — a mention of my father never fails to earn a warm round of spontaneous applause.

"You see, although my father had desperately wanted to make Sooty international himself, he was absolutely delighted that I have been able to achieve it to a certain extent. That's why I get annoyed when newspapers in this country quote me as saying that basically he was jealous because I'm the one who has made Sooty international. They imply that because of that we didn't get on. That's rubbish. My son Ben has more 'O' Levels than I have and I am 'jealous' of that — but at the same time, I'm proud as hell of him and I love him the more for it. So it was with my father — he was one hundred and one per cent behind me."

Sooty has become such big business in the Southern Hemisphere that since 1982, when Matthew embarked on his inaugural five-week tour of New Zealand

and Australia, Arnold Fry has regularly arranged for Sooty to go Down Under. Before that first tour, Matthew decided that a good way of attracting publicity and even credibility was to have his photo taken with an Australian megastar. Since Skippy wasn't available, he settled for housewife superstar Dame Edna Everage, alias Barry Humphries. "I approached Barry after a performance of Dame Edna's one-woman show at the Strand Theatre in London's West End.

"I said: 'I'd like to do a photo of the two of us to help me in Australia. Would you mind being photographed with me?

"'Not at all,' he replied, adding, 'and I'm sure Dame Edna will be delighted as well. I'm sure she's a big fan.'

"I thought: 'This is a bit strange.' But he went out, came back as Dame Edna and it was as if we had never met before. Barry is two different people. As Dame Edna would say: 'It was kinda spooky.'"

While in Australia, Sooty had another of those unfortunate experiences he has endured from time to time at the hands of animals. On this particular occasion, he suffered grievous bodily harm from a koala. "We thought it a good idea for one bear to meet another," says Matthew, "and since I didn't fancy tangling with a polar bear, we plumped for a koala at Melbourne Zoo. The koala was very interested in Sooty but having put its arm around him, he must have decided that Sooty's head was actually a furry fruit because he proceeded to take a large bite out of him!"

Needless to say, Matthew has suffered further moments of discomfort when disobeying the old showbusiness adage about never working with animals. A marmoset monkey once climbed on his head and made its feelings quite clear, leaving Matthew to change a soaking wet shirt again — only this time it had nothing to do with Sooty's water-pistol.

And a fate too awful to contemplate nearly befell Sooty when he was introduced to an elephant at

147

Chessington Zoo. "The elephant tried to lift Sooty out of his basket," recalls Matthew, "but there was a problem because I was on the end of Sooty. When I've got Sooty on, where he goes, I go. I think the elephant was quite surprised to discover that Sooty weighed twelve stone."

On the same occasion, Sooty was to be filmed making a plasticine model of an elephant and displaying it in front of the animals. Unfortunately the elephant decided that the model looked like a tasty morsel, hooked it up with its trunk and promptly ate it. The keeper was justifiably furious and had to give the elephant no fewer than ten gallons of beer to act as a laxative and wash the plasticine out of the creature's system. So if you ever see an elephant with a hangover, you'll know it's probably something he's eaten.

For a programme shot at the Metropolitan Police Dog Training Centre in Kent, Matthew had arranged for a special remote-controlled Sooty to be constructed. The idea was that this technologically-advanced Sooty would be placed at the end of the narrow eighteen-inch tube through which the dogs run as part of their training. However, far from the anticipated lick and wag of a tail, the first alsatian to emerge from the tube immediately snapped at Sooty and started to savage him. He would have been chewed into little pieces but for the intervention of the handlers, who managed to prise the mangled body out of the dog's jaws. A few weeks after that incident, Matthew had good reason for taking a permanent dislike to alsatians when he himself was attacked by a friend's German Shepherds. And they say a dog is man's best friend. Try telling Matthew Corbett.

On the face of it, filming *The Sooty Show* should not really require the presence of a stunt man. Matthew is not often seen scaling cliffs, shooting rapids or parascending. . . all because Soo loves Milk Tray. But he did manage to injure himself once when competing in a running race against Sooty. He contrived to fall down a hole , damaging his back in the process, and he still feels considerable pain four years later. Sometimes I feel Sooty has a lot to answer for.

Apart from conquering the world with Sooty, Matthew's other principal ambition, again one shared by his father, has been to play the mecca of British entertainment, the London Palladium. But so far that dream has remained unfulfilled. "It's been a real thorn in my side," confesses Matthew. "Twice I thought I'd cracked it. The first time was when Rod Hull asked me whether I'd pop along and do something in the *Children's Royal Variety Performance*. I said that I would be delighted. Then shortly afterwards, I received a long letter of apology from Rod telling me that the management, headed by Louis Benjamin, didn't want Sooty. Rod felt awful. He said: 'I'm so embarrassed I don't know what to say.'

"The second let-down came after John Fisher, a producer at the BBC with whom I had worked when Sooty had appeared on *Wogan* and *The Paul Daniels Show*, rang me up another year about the *Children's Royal Variety Performance*.

"He said: 'We've got a Disney sequence in the show called "Talk to the Animals". I wondered whether you'd just like to walk on during that.'

"'That's very kind of you, John, but I wish maybe you had said: 'Why don't you come on and do an act?'

"'But surely you're bored with doing that? You must have done it so many times.'

"'Well actually, John, I've never done that.'

"'You've never done the *Children's Royal Variety*?'

"'Never.'

"'I can hardly believe that,' he said.

"So Sooty and I were set to sing in this Disney sequence. All the dates were fixed and then at the eleventh hour the Disney people stated that they wouldn't allow any other characters (in other words non-Disney) to be associated with their part of the show. So we missed out again.

"I said to John Fisher: 'It's come to something when an American organisation is dictating to us Brits what we will have in our *Children's Royal Variety Performance*.'

"'I agree with you,' he said, 'but I can't change it. It's too late — the show's happening next week.' Then he added: 'I'm so embarrassed I don't know what to say. . .'

"I said: 'John, I've been here before. . .'

"It just shows the politics that goes on behind the scenes of these events. It means that Sooty, the number one children's show, has never done the *Royal Variety*, which is supposed to be for children. It seems extraordinary to me."

Sooty may have missed out on the *Royal Variety* but he is still heavily involved in other charity work. The blind boxes continue to pop up in the most unexpected places, most recently on the bar of the Rovers Return in *Coronation Street*! Matthew believes this could be the work of actor Bryan Mosley, who plays corner shopkeeper Alf Roberts and who once appeared in repertory with Matthew at Scarborough.

"Bryan was a notorious practical joker. When we were doing *Spring and Port Wine* and trying to act terribly sensibly, Bryan was lurking in the wings dangling a plastic pixie on a nylon thread down the side of the set and reducing us all to hysterics. One of the cast solved the immediate problem by breaking the thread, but that merely resulted in this wretched pixie being furtively passed among us on stage while the audience, totally oblivious to what was going on, watched what was supposed to be an extremely serious scene. When Bryan, who played father, entered I thought I'd get my own back on him by dropping the pixie into his cup of tea. But he took it all in his stride and simply drank the lot, delivering his next line with a mouthful of pixie before making an unscheduled exit. Moments later he returned to the stage adjusting his trousers and announced, 'That's better.' I'm afraid it was too much for the rest of us. We just corpsed."

Sooty also makes a lot of personal appearances at special schools and children's homes and managed to raise £20,000 for Ethiopia. It is a far cry from one of his first charity ventures when in 1956 the Lord's Day Observance Society barred Harry and Sooty from appearing in a Sunday show at the Theatre Royal, Huddersfield, in aid of the Hungarian Relief Fund.

For over twenty years, Sooty has brought his own special brand of magic to brighten up the lives of hundreds of physically handicapped youngsters at a special school near Mansfield in Nottinghamshire. Every December, while his stage show is appearing at Mansfield's Civic Centre, Sooty goes along to perform at Fountaindale School's Christmas Party and even presents an annual Sooty Kindness Cup to the child who has given most to the others in the school over the previous year. It is a tradition that was started by Harry Corbett when the school was known as Park Hall and has been continued by Matthew ever since. Until he retired last year, the headmaster first at Park Hall and then at Fountaindale was Ray Newnes.

He says: "It all began when the manager at the Civic Theatre introduced me to Harry one year. I told him about the school and he was only too happy to come along and do a show for us. I remember he and Marjorie used to park their touring caravan on the lawn of a nearby pub. He only ever missed one Christmas dinner and that was as a result of a mix-up over the date and even then he turned up the following day so we had one then as well. The party became a fixture in both our diaries. He said to me once: 'Ray, if I did my week at Mansfield in July, would you have your Christmas dinner then?' And the answer would have been 'yes'. We would have done anything to accommodate Sooty. The great thing is that Matthew has carried on in the same vein. He and Sallie actually stay at the school for the week that they're in Mansfield and he has become tremendous friends with the children, particularly the older ones, because some of the pupils are as old as thirty. Even though Sooty is supposed to appeal mainly to the young, you can bet that there is hardly a conversation with these twenty or thirty-year-olds without some mention of Sooty. He has become the centrepiece of their lives. He has given them something to hang on to. Most theatres can't cater for disabled youngsters, so this has been the first chance these pupils have had to associate with a top television personality. It's lovely that we've been able to put this into their lives and the joy on their faces when they meet Sooty is indescribable. Matthew and Sooty have virtually become part of the school and their visit is something that everyone looks forward to immensely.

"Over the years I have managed to attract many celebrities to Fountaindale — Sir Harry Secombe, Lulu, Des O'Connor, Little and Large — as well as Prince Charles, Princess Diana and, only last year, the Duchess of York. But at the risk of offending the Royal Family, I would definitely say that Sooty is the main attraction. He's number one.

"Probably part of the reason why the pupils look forward to Sooty's party," admits Ray, "is that something diabolical always happens to me. I can't remember a Christmas Dinner when I didn't have to change my shirt half-way through. What made it worse was that Matthew never told me what was going to happen. I always got my come-uppance though whether it was from jugs of custard, pies or the dreaded water-pistol which Matthew somehow rigged so that the water came out in an absolute torrent."

It was Matthew's turn to suffer one year, however. "Matthew used to be a bit of a show-off when it came to cars," says Ray, "and his pride and joy was this flashy red Mercedes. All the kids admired it but when it was time to leave, it wouldn't start. And because there was no Mercedes dealer locally, to everyone's utter delight, this expensive-looking status symbol had to be carted off ignominiously on a tatty low loader. Everyone cheered wildly — it really cut poor Matthew down to size!"

Matthew himself says: "Fountaindale is the nicest place I've ever been to. It is a wonderful caring environment. Those kids meant a lot to my father and they do to me. And it's always very sad when I learn that one of them who I've probably known for years has died. My daughter Tamsin was so impressed by the school and by what those youngsters can do in wheelchairs that she decided that all she wanted for Christmas one year was a wheelchair. It really is a remarkable place."

Matthew is not likely to forget the 1982 trip to Mansfield in a hurry because it was then that Sallie was rushed to hospital with a brain haemorrhage. He recalls: "I was doing the show at the Civic when I heard that Sallie had been taken to hospital in London. It was the only time I've ever walked out on the show. I told the theatre: 'I don't care. You can sue me, you can do what you like, I'm not staying. I can't be here in Mansfield while my wife is undergoing brain surgery in London.' But in my absence everyone rallied round. My valuable sidekick Connie Creighton took over and they re-wrote the stage show in Ray Newnes' living-room. And Connie took Sooty to the Fountaindale party that year. So although I wasn't there, the show did go on. I just had to be with Sallie who completely recovered. But actually it did wonders for our marriage, because it proved conclusively to Sallie that she was more important to me than Sooty."

Because of his commitments in Australia and a desire to spend at least some time with his family, Matthew, like Sooty, has started employing stand-ins for part of the stage tour. A popular presenter of the Sooty stage show is the aforementioned Connie Creighton, who first worked with Harry back in 1974 as a support act. "I'm a children's entertainer in my own right," says Connie, "and I used to do my act, some quick-draw cartooning and a little bit of magic, while the scenery was being changed during the Sooty Show. One day, Harry asked Vincent Shaw to come and watch me at a children's birthday party with a view to my working with Sooty on a more permanent basis. It was one of those occasions when everything went wrong, the children didn't do anything they were told, it was chaotic.

"I thought: 'Oh, I've definitely blown it.'

"But Vincent said: 'If you can cope with all that, then you're the girl for us.'

"I was something of a novelty at the time because I was the first female guest artist to have appeared with Sooty and people felt that you couldn't squirt a woman with water or shove a custard pie in her face. I proved them wrong."

As a girl, Connie was an ardent Sooty fan and declares that her life-long ambition was to work with him. (At least it makes a change from wanting to travel the world and meet people). "I usually take out the second half of the tour," says Connie, "although last year for the first time I presented some of the pre-Christmas shows too while Matthew was preparing for Australia. When I started, I was very aware of having to keep up this great Corbett tradition. It was a daunting prospect having to step into their shoes. But I've found that as long as the children like you, you're OK."

One of Connie's most memorable experiences occurred in her very first year with Sooty when she managed to find one of the few people in the world who had never heard of the little bear. "We were doing a show somewhere up in the north-east and on the Saturday we had to do three performances. On the Saturday morning I woke up with a horrible bloodshot eye. I hadn't a clue what had caused it. With the aid of heavy make-up, I got through the first performance but it was so bad that the stage manager advised me to go along to the casualty department at the local hospital. The doctor was Asian.

"'What do you do for a living?' he asked

"'I'm with Sooty,' I replied.

"'What is Sooty?'

"'A yellow bear.'

"'Oh, you work with animals. You must have an anti-tetanus jab!'

"I couldn't convince him that Sooty was only a puppet until the nurses explained it to him. I really did think I was going to get an anti-tetanus jab for working with Sooty. . ."

Sooty still has plenty of unusual fans. At the 1988 Farnborough Air Show, police directing the traffic donned Sooty, Sweep and Soo puppets to keep frustrated motorists amused while they sat in traffic jams. It just goes to show, the long arm of the law really does get everywhere.

And Connie Creighton reveals that Sooty has built up a cult following among students. "When it was Sooty's fortieth birthday in 1988, we offered a bottle of champagne to anyone who brought along a birth certificate to prove that they too were forty. These students from Southport turned up with fake certificates and really early Sooty puppets. In fact one puppet was so worn on the top of his head that somebody had made a wig for him. I'm sure Harry never visualised Sooty in dreadlocks!"

In spite of this adult adulation, it's still children that can be relied upon to provide prize comments. Sooty's 1988 stage tour was a powerful production entitled *Sooty in Space*, but Connie remembers a moment when the tension was marred somewhat by a young boy. "In the show, Sweep was launched into space and everyone in the cast had to pretend to be deeply worried about him because he was nowhere to be found. There was then a fifteen-minute interval, during which the whole audience would be kept in suspense, before Sweep was eventually discovered safely on Mars. But one day just as we were at the most dramatic part, all wondering what had happened to Sweep, the tense silence was broken by a little Cockney voice from the audience piping up: 'Oi, he's copped it, mister.'"

Bearing in mind all the doubts that existed in the Sixties with entrepreneurs declaring that a Sooty stage show would never work, it is worth noting that Vincent Shaw says he can now book a full tour of thirty-eight weeks in just twenty minutes. Sooty has become a tradition in certain towns and venues which means that virtually every performance on the tour is a sell-out with children dragging their parents (and vice-versa) from miles around. It wasn't until I went to see *Sooty's Circus* last year and saw him balancing on the tightrope that I realised he had acquired something he never appeared to have in the old days — legs. However most of the time he is still seen just from the waist up and only puts his legs on for special occasions. He must therefore lay claim to being the world's only bionic bear.

Apart from Sooty gaining extra limbs, throughout the Eighties the shows became increasingly sophisticated. Matthew tries to think up a new theme for each year's tour and over the past few years has produced and directed such box-office blockbusters as *Starpaws, Sooty's Circus, The House That Sooty Built, Sooty's Wild West Show* and *Sooty's World Cruise*. One of the most spectacular sets was a magnificent boat, the Saucy Sooty, which cost in excess of £5,000 and weighed more than two tons. The audiences loved it but it wasn't as popular with the stage crews who often had to dismantle it every day over a period of eight months.

One show nearly ended in disaster when the long cable of Matthew's microphone became entangled with Sooty, garrotting him in the process. So wherever Matthew moved across the stage, he inadvertently dragged the strangled Sooty with him. "I had to say to the audience: 'See how human he is, he even follows me around!'"

Worse still was the occasion when, horror of horrors, Sooty was stolen shortly before a performance at Croydon, Surrey. Matthew remembers: "When we arrived on the Saturday morning to do the show, we discovered that the actual Sooty, Sweep and Soo puppets we were going to use on stage had gone along with a box of some two hundred Sootys which were to go on sale to the public. Even though I assured them it was a genuine theft, the theatre was convinced it was all a big publicity stunt, particularly as television and the newspapers quickly latched on to the story. We managed to get through that day's performances by using spare puppets although we had to reassure the children in the audience that these were the originals and that only Sooty's understudies had been taken. Otherwise the kids would have had nightmares worrying about the real Sooty being stolen. The papers made a great fuss, demanding to know how anyone could be so heartless as to steal the very puppets that were about to entertain hundreds of children. It proved to be another triumph for the British Press for a couple of days later Sooty, Sweep and Soo were left in a carrier bag on the step of a Surrey police station with a note attached which read: 'Sorry, we didn't realise these were the ones you used in the show.' As for the other two hundred, I gather they appeared in street markets, selling at two quid a head. To ensure there were no further attempts to kidnap him, Sooty arrived at Bradford the following week in a security van. Now that was a publicity stunt."

Another terrifying ordeal for Sooty was when he spent an hour and a half on the run in Manchester. Matthew explains: "A mate and I had caught a taxi from the station to my friend's house in Manchester and after a couple of minutes he said to me: 'Where's your case?' I realised that I'd left it in the taxi and it was no ordinary case because it contained the special box marked Sooty on the front and inside was Sooty himself, his magic wand and his water-pistol. It was the box I used for all my personal appearances. I was lost without it. I rushed outside in the hope that the taxi might still be there but needless to say it had gone. Neither of us had a clue what taxi firm we'd used, we had just jumped in the first one that came along at the station. I was going spare. So we had to ring round every taxi firm in Manchester at 11.30 at night.

"I'd say: 'I'm dreadfully sorry but I've left Sooty in the back of a taxi. Is it one of yours?'

"And the bloke on the other end answers: 'Oh yeah, and I'm the Queen of Sheba. . .'

"Even the police didn't believe me. You couldn't really blame people — at that time of night, they must have thought we were a couple of drunks playing a practical joke. Finally, we tracked down the right firm and they brought Sooty back safely. But I really did think I'd lost him for good and that he was going to end up on someone's mantelpiece in Manchester."

However there are two Sootys that have never been recovered. One was an ornamental stone Sooty which, together with his Sweep counterpart, was stolen from Harry Corbett's front garden in Dorset, and the other was a giant four-foot tall version, made in fibre glass and covered in fur, that Harry had used for a summer season at a model village in Southport back in the Sixties. The outsize bear was strapped to the roof of Harry's Land Rover outside a Southport restaurant but was untied by ruthless villains and, despite a nationwide alert, has never been seen since. So for nigh on thirty years, somebody somewhere has been gazing at a massive Sooty in their home. What can have become of him? Is he in the corner of a lounge as a standard lamp or does he adorn a patio with trailing fuschias growing out of his eyes, ears and other strategic places? It doesn't bear thinking about, does it?

CHAPTER EIGHT

BYE BYE EVERYBODY, BYE BYE

While Matthew was maintaining the great Sooty tradition and steering him successfully through the Eighties, down in Dorset Harry Corbett was still keeping his hand in. After twenty-five years of non-stop work, the traumas of the heart attack and the agonies of coming to terms with losing Sooty, Harry was entitled to spend the rest of his years in peace. But despite his initial frailty, he still possessed a stubborn determination to resume doing Sooty on a professional basis and this, of course, resulted in the clash with Matthew. In some ways, the family friction turned out to be a blessing because it made Harry realise just how carefully he had to tread in future. No matter how much he recovered physically, he couldn't carry on the same way as before. Matthew was in charge now, whether Harry liked it or not.

And in truth, Harry did like it. Once he'd got doing Sooty "properly", as he termed it, out of his system, he was delighted to just concentrate on doing little local shows on a part-time basis while leaving Matthew to suffer all the headaches involved with television and touring. Eventually, Harry cut out doing provincial theatres, arts centres, even fetes and settled for doing an eight-week summer season near his home, in somewhere like Weymouth or Bournemouth, plus one show near Christmas.

"That way I had a little bit of spending money without too much hassle. It was a perfect arrangement."

The other way in which Harry remained firmly involved with Sooty was by building props for Matthew in his workshop at Child Okeford. The cottage was originally a farmhouse and Harry's workshop was a converted pig-sty. "It all really started with the grandfather clock I made Matthew not that long after my heart attack. While waiting for it to be delivered to him, it stood proudly in our lounge for a few weeks and when it was gone, it left an empty space. So Marj asked me if I would make one for her and I built another grandfather clock, this time in Japanese oak with a glass door. All of this must have registered with Matthew that the old feller's rather handy in the workshop and he asked me whether I would make him something for the show."

Harry didn't need any persuading. It was just what he wanted. It enabled him to feel a genuine part of *The Sooty Show* again but without the strain and pressure of yesteryear. "I don't know whether Matthew planned to give me work to get me going again but if he did, it was the ideal therapy. Once I got going in the workshop, I forgot all about my depression at not doing Sooty full-time any more. It was the perfect thing to occupy my mind."

Harry was soon hard at work. One of his first tasks was to build a special bedroom with no floor and with holes in the mattress so that the manipulator could get Sooty into bed with Matthew. Marjorie says: "The nice thing was that Harry understood all this. If you said to anybody else, 'build me a bedroom without a floor', they wouldn't have a clue what to do. They wouldn't know how to fit things in. But Harry was used to it so he was able to be a tremendous help to Matthew. Mind you, I had to keep a firm hand on him. He was working seven days a week again until I put my foot down and said: 'Look sunshine, there's more to life than work.' You see, once he got his teeth into something, there was no stopping him. I'm very much against the wife being neglected and at that time I thought I wasn't getting the attention I deserved. I also had to watch he didn't take on too many shows for us, not only because we didn't want to cut across Matthew again but also for Harry's own sake. After all, he had suffered a devastating heart attack and it was a long, slow haul to recovery. So sometimes when he came up with a booking, I had to put my foot down and say: 'No Harry, we can't do that.'"

Harry's activities didn't necessarily please his doctors either. Remember that in 1976 he'd been told he might live for another fifteen years but only if he slowed right down. Harry didn't agree with that diagnosis. "Some doctors who more or less said: 'Don't do anything, take it easy' were entirely wrong. I think it should have been the other way round. They should have advised: 'Do as much as you possibly can, keep the muscles going, you'll know when you're too tired and that's the time to stop.' I surprised myself with what I could do. Never for one moment did I think I could build grandfather clocks or some of the things I made for the show like those circus stunt cars that fall apart bit by bit and ships, robots and rockets."

When I visited Harry and Marjorie in June, 1989, the space rocket was his pride and joy. He was just putting the finishing touches to it, ready for delivery to Matthew for his next stage show in the autumn. It was a masterpiece of construction — even a hard taskmaster like Bill Garrett would have been proud of it. Harry's handywork was much in evidence around the home. Besides the grandfather clock, he had built cupboards, a bookcase, a sewing box and for the grandchildren, a splendid dolls' house. Another proud exhibit, although not of course one built by Harry, was the same Steinway piano that he played so brilliantly as a youngster and which used to swamp the sitting-room of the little house in Guiseley where he and Marjorie started out on married life. While on the subject of Harry's diverse accomplishments, he was also a talented artist and once had a self-portrait included in an exhibition of paintings by stage and screen personalities. He was far more than just a puppeteer.

The Corbetts' thatched cottage in the heart of the beautiful Dorset countryside is a local landmark. Villagers refer to it as "Sooty's house" and naturally it became a magnet for children from the surrounding area. Harry would never disappoint them, no matter how inconvenient their timing. "I could be right in the middle of something and there'd be a knock on the door and a brother and sister standing there asking: 'Where's Sooty?' I remember once I was so busy that I was completely stumped for a reply so off the top of my head for some reason I said: 'He's gone to look for some worms.' They rushed off and ten minutes later returned gleefully clutching a jar of worms. This time I had to produce Sooty so I brought him down and he thanked them, gave them a kiss and they ran off happily. And I was left with a jar of worms!"

There were always plenty of Sootys for Harry to choose from around the house. In addition to the supply he kept for his summer seasons and past cast-offs which he auctioned for charity, Sooty, Sweep and Soo puppets sit perched at the window of the main bedroom, looking out at passers-by, as if wondering how the world has changed in their lifetimes. And everywhere there are assorted teddy bears in all shapes and sizes. "I adore teddy bears," said Harry. "I think much of the reason for Sooty's success is that the most lovable character in the world is the teddy bear. And everyone loves dogs like Sweep too. So Sooty and Sweep are the perfect combination." But when it comes to choosing between the two, Harry was in no doubt as to where his loyalties lied. "Over the years, the ratio of glove puppet sales in theatres after the shows has been that for every ten Sootys, we have sold five Sweeps and three Soos. Some people think Sweep is the star of the show but he isn't. Sooty is number one."

Even after forty years together, Harry was still utterly devoted to his creation. In a Mills and Boon book, it would have been a partnership made in Heaven. He told me: "Not only is Sooty part of the family but I often even find myself wondering what he's thinking. It's as bad as that. Before every show, I wash his face and brush his fur. If I accidentally drop him, I immediately apologise. And if I catch anybody throwing him around carelessly, I don't hesitate to tell them off. I know it sounds ridiculous regarding Sooty as a person because he's really only two fingers on my right hand but I can't help it. If you look back at the old black and white programmes, you can see the affection between the puppets and myself on screen. You can see that I think they're real.

"The worst thing is having to break in a new Sooty puppet. It's always difficult starting with a new one because they're never quite the same. I think of it as a new partner who doesn't know me yet. I get so anxious I come out in beads of sweat. And I feel terrible about the one I've just discarded — I've actually apologised to them when I've taken them off and replaced them. I carefully put the old one into a box and say: 'I'm sorry but I'm not using you again.' It makes me feel awful. I'm so bloody soft at times."

When Harry and Marjorie presented their own stage show in the Eighties, it was slightly different from the one seen on TV with Matthew. It was very much their interpretation of Sooty, the way they had always envisaged the characters. Soo, in particular, was not as bossy as on television — she had reverted to her original personality of Miss Goody Two Shoes. And Sooty, operated by Harry, was always courtesy itself to Soo, manipulated by Marjorie. In many respects, the puppets' friendship reflected the real-life closeness between husband and wife. "I'd never allow Sooty to stick a flower-pot on Soo's nose without apologising," admitted Harry. In the same way, I'm sure Harry would never have stuck a flower-pot on Marjorie's nose without apologising.

Harry laughed off suggestions that in reality Sooty and Soo have been living in sin for the past twenty-five years, a promiscuous product of the Swinging Sixties. "No matter how old they are in material terms, they're five and four to me. And in spite of what the BBC thought, their relationship has always been perfectly innocent. They're just good friends — they have never known anything about sex."

The Corbetts rarely missed *The Sooty Show* on television. "I think Matthew has done a wonderful job," said Harry. "We both thoroughly enjoy the show, it is well-presented and colourful. I tend to watch Sooty while Marjorie watches Soo. Mind you, we're critical sometimes, particularly about the puppets." The principal cause for concern was poor old Sweep, who these days looks at best as if he's had a face-lift and at worst as if his head has been squashed in a giant vice. Neither Harry, nor his brother Leslie, who operated Sweep for ten years, approved of the new-look hound.

Harry said: "I used to tell Matthew, 'I don't think much of the Sweep puppet at the moment. His face is all wrong.'

"He'd say: 'Well nobody's complained.'

"I said: 'Well I am.'

"I reckon the toughest thing of all has been getting a Sooty or Sweep made which pleases me. So Matthew always knew it was a real compliment if I said that not only did I enjoy the show but it was a good Sooty this week too."

Devotees will also have noticed that Soo's voice has dropped an octave or two since her controversial introduction in the Sixties. Whereas she always used to sound as if she was sitting on something painful, these days her tones are much deeper. It is of course nothing gynaecological, merely that Marjorie's successor Brenda

Longman chooses not to hit the high notes.

In the comfort of his own home, Harry was a fund of reminiscences about his unique career. True his memory had become a little blurred in certain areas but he could still remember the precise details of virtually every Sooty story-line. The only outward signs of the near-fatal heart attack were the necessity to take a short nap in the afternoon (which at seventy-one he was entitled to anyway) and the occasional tendency to stumble over long words. Nobody could ever say success had changed Harry — he remained a down-to-earth Yorkshireman who eagerly looked forward to driving his wife to a local pub for a fish and chip supper every Thursday evening. Like Sooty, fish and chips were in Harry's blood. A man of simple pleasures, he was at peace with the world (Marjorie described him as "gentle, smiling and fulfilled") and there was nothing he liked more than recollecting how adults had fallen under the spell of the little bear with the magic wand. One of his favourite yarns concerned the occasion back in the 1960s when Sooty was booked by the editor of the *Daily Express* to entertain the illustrious Circuit Club who met once a month at Claridge's in London.

"I've found that adults love Sooty as much as children do, men even more so than women. Men really are the softest creatures on Earth and I think the reason they adore Sooty is because he takes them back to their childhood. This Circuit Club at Claridge's was a very posh affair. We were down to do the cabaret at 11pm after Harry Worth. When we came on stage, there were all these lords and sirs, sitting in their medals and full regalia and knocking back brandies and smoking foot-long cigars after a sumptuous meal. I thought to myself: 'What the hell's Sooty doing at a place like this?'

"I had perfected the art of enabling Sooty to put his little black spectacles on by himself without any visible help from me. He did this and proceeded to survey the audience. I told them: 'Sooty says he won't do a thing unless you all wave to him.' So they all put down their cigars, their faces beamed and they waved back. From then on it was just brilliant. I said: 'He wants you to say the magic spell, 'Izzy Whizzy, Let's Get Busy' and there's all of these lords and judges chanting 'Izzy Whizzy, Let's Get Busy'. It was unbelievable. Afterwards, they came up and said it was the best cabaret they'd had in the history of the club. One member was a head of CID. He suggested: 'Why don't you have a programme with Sooty as a detective? I'll show you round Scotland Yard if you like and give you all the inside information on finger-printing.' All that privileged access — just for Sooty. With that knowledge, he could have become an arch criminal! It was the most remarkable transformation I've ever seen in my life — those highly-respected members of society were just like thirty schoolkids that night.

"People are usually very kind about Sooty. It's always gratifying when someone you've never met before comes up to you and says sincerely: 'Long may Sooty continue.' He's held in such tremendous affection and it never ceases to amaze me that even when Marjorie and I go on holiday abroad, I'm still recognised even though I haven't been doing the show on television for years. I remember I was driving along in Copenhagen and when we stopped at a set of traffic lights, another car pulled up alongside and some lads leaned over and asked: 'Where's Sooty?' And when we were in Austria, a woman looked me up and down and said: 'Don't I know you from somewhere?' I quite enjoy being recognised but sometimes, out of devilment I suppose, I lead people on for a while and pretend I'm not Harry Corbett at all, that I just look a bit like him. Marjorie gets very cross with me then but I'm only playing about — I always confess in the end. Out of all the accolades I've received, I think the highest praise came from an old boy in a northern pub. He walked over to me and said: 'I don't want to interrupt. I've only one thing to say — thy stuff's acceptable.' Coming from a

Yorkshire working man in a flat cap, that's the greatest compliment of all."

Not everyone was as appreciative of Sooty. Harry recalled a brush with comedian Terry Scott on a television programme in Plymouth. "It was like a chat show," said Harry, "and Sooty and I were sitting next to Terry Scott. Because of the success of *Terry and June*, I think he considered himself to be above Harry Corbett and Sooty. He was full of himself but Sooty was there beside him and completely stole the show. The audience reacted to him not Scott who had all the wind taken out of his sails. He was totally put off by Sooty — he just didn't know how to handle the situation. I don't think he was too pleased."

It was Harry's turn to be displeased when he was invited to open the River Carnival at Wimborne, one of the biggest in Dorset. "I've been asked to do some funny things in my time, like that football match at Blackpool, and I remember once Sooty even opened the Highland Games. Goodness knows why they chose Sooty! You never know what you're letting yourself in for when you make these personal appearances, and Wimborne was a prime example. At the time, I was appearing on Bournemouth pier doing a morning show at 11.0 and an afternoon performance at 2.30. The organiser wanted me to open the carnival in my lunch hour.

"I said: 'There's no time. The 11.0 show doesn't finish until 12.30 and I've got to be back for half-past two. There's no way I can get to Wimborne and back in that time.'

"'You can manage it,' insisted the guy in charge. 'I'll meet you at the end of the pier and we'll take a short cut to Wimborne.'

"Against my better judgement, he talked me into it. When we arrived at Wimborne, there were masses of people all packed on one side of the river which was really wide at that spot, about a hundred yards across.

"'Right,' I said, 'where are we doing it?'

"'Over there, on the other side of the river. On that platform. Can you see it?'

"And there in the distance, right across the river in a field was this little platform.

"I said: 'I can't do it there.'

"'Why not? Others have.'

"'But they haven't got a little puppet. Nobody will be able to see Sooty and I over there.'

"'I hadn't thought of that. . .'

"I had no choice. I couldn't pull out. So I had to try and do the best I could. If they couldn't see Sooty, it was too bad.

"'How are we going to cross the river?' I queried.

"'In a rowing boat,' came the reply.

"So in front of five thousand people, I climbed into a rowing boat with Sooty and my props and this chap took us across.

"When we got to the other side, I said: 'I need a bit of time to set everything up. Is there somewhere I can go where nobody can see what I'm doing?'

"'You could go behind that tree.'

"'Is there a microphone stand?' I asked.

"'No but there's a hand microphone that you can pick up.'

"'But if I've got Sooty on one hand and I'm doing a bit of business or a magic trick with the other, I won't be able to pick it up.'

"'Well, have someone standing at the side of you.'

"'I don't want someone standing right next to me. . .'

"In the end, we tied the microphone to a broom handle and planted it in the soil. I set my box up behind the tree and did a show on this rickety old platform where the crowd needed binoculars to see me. It was ridiculous. And they say showbusiness is glamorous."

Harry also regretted fulfilling an engagement in Yorkshire where the organiser of a television show wanted everyone in the audience to put on a Sooty puppet. "He wanted it for effect but I wasn't at all happy about it. For a start, seeing all those Sootys destroys the illusion for kiddies. They think there's only one Sooty. Also, the people in the audience didn't know how to work Sooty properly. There's more to it than just sticking him on your hand. At first, I said I wasn't going to allow it but in the end I gave in. I wish I hadn't because when I looked out, there were rows and rows of crippled-looking Sootys where people were straining to hold the puppets correctly. It was an awful experience."

Even in semi-retirement, Harry's whole life revolved around Sooty. With no puppet in sight, he would think nothing of going through a whole routine with his bare fingers, his voice frequently rising to that high-pitched Yorkshire agitation which usually preceeded his face being squirted with ink and which lit up my Sunday afternoons in the Fifties. Such behaviour used to drive Matthew to distraction. "I used to get so embarrassed when he started doing a show in a pub or a restaurant with his fingers. I just couldn't believe what he was doing!"

Leslie Corbett recalls going to see his brother for a chat one Christmas. "Harry was sitting at the fireside with the script of his Christmas show and he'd got Sooty on. We were just talking about various things, not about the show, and out of the corner of my eye I could see Sooty nodding away, following the entire conversation. I'm absolutely sure Harry didn't know he was doing that. It was just something he did automatically without realising it."

"When I was doing Sooty full-time, I used to concentrate five hundred per cent on the programme," said Harry. "I would often be in a complete world of my own around the house, oblivious to everything that was going on. I remember once I went down to the cellar to fetch a bucket full of coal. I came up again, passed the lounge where the fire was and went up another flight of stairs into the bathroom. I was just about to empty the coal scuttle down the toilet when I suddenly came round. 'What the hell am I doing here?' I thought and managed to stop myself right in the nick of time.

"On another occasion, we were due to go out for dinner with a couple of friends. I went upstairs to change and came down ready to go to the restaurant. 'What on earth are you doing?' screamed Marjorie. I looked down and realised I was standing in there in my pyjamas. I was so intense thinking what I was going to be doing on the next show that I had changed into my pyjamas by mistake!"

Marjorie was invaluable to Harry throughout his career. Besides being a tremendous emotional support, working Soo, making the puppets' clothes and generally assisting on stage, she often had to provide Harry with props for Sooty's various pranks. But there was one instance when she got it wrong and she has never been allowed to live it down. "I wanted an egg for one of Sooty's tricks," said Harry. "We had a housekeeper at the time and she did a hard-boiled egg for Matthew's breakfast. But he then changed his mind and ate something else so Marjorie put the hard-boiled egg next to the basket of ordinary eggs. Just as we were about to leave to do the show, and this was in the days of live television, I reminded Marj: 'Don't forget an egg to put under my hat.' So she chose six beautiful eggs, the best from the basket. I duly went through the whole routine on TV and ended up with an egg under my schoolboy cap. The idea was that Sooty would bash the egg and it would come sliding down my face. But when Sooty hit me with the hammer, nothing happened. I waited in vain for the egg to dribble down. Then I lifted my cap and gave it another bash. Still nothing. The egg just went bonk. Sooty had a look, I had a look and in the end I just said: 'Bye bye everybody, bye bye.' When I examined the egg, I discovered that it was hard-boiled.

No wonder it wouldn't crack. 'How on earth did that happen?' I moaned. We later found out that the housekeeper had put the hard-boiled egg back in the basket with the others and by sheer misfortune, Marjorie had picked that very one for the show. For once, I wasn't left with egg on my face — but Marjorie was."

Another member of the Corbett household who used to get in on the act was Blossom, their little papillon dog. But she once took the theatrical good luck greeting of "break a leg" too literally. Her main role was to pop out of Bill Garrett's specially-made xylophone to the strains of "How Much Is That Doggie in the Window?" After that, she would jump off the table into Marjorie's waiting arms. "But one time on Bournemouth pier," recalled Harry, "Blossom jumped too soon, missed Marjorie and fell five foot on to the stage. She screamed the place down so we hurried her off to a vet who told us that she had dislocated her knee. We were horrified. Still the show had to go on so we went out and bought a kitten substitute and changed the tune to "I Tought I Taw a Puddy Tat". The only problem was the kitten was so small she was able to poke her head through the keys of the xylophone which rather spoiled the surprise. The animals became great pals at home and we used to roar laughing watching the kitten try and trip up the poor three-legged dog.

"Also part of the stage act was a friendly little parakeet which used to perch on my finger and kiss me. We carried it around in a box and unfortunately this assistant we had seemed to take great pleasure in vigorously shaking the box to make sure the bird was safely inside. After a few such shakings, naturally enough the bird became annoyed and instead of standing there gently it gave my finger a sharp peck. In view of this, I decided it was safer to pick it up with the magic wand next time but the bird promptly raced along the wand and sank its beak into the same finger!"

In December 1988, Harry had received one

of television's ultimate accolades — he was the subject of *This Is Your Life*. It was a case of third time lucky since Harry had been selected as a victim twice before but on both occasions the programme had fallen through. The first time was back in the Seventies but the production researchers had received little encouragement from Marjorie. "Much as I loved him, to me Harry was just an ordinary man," she says. "I wasn't being unhelpful but I suppose I didn't really come up with any wonderful stories about him and they obviously didn't think there was sufficient material to make a show." The second time, in 1987, they did obtain plenty of anecdotes and it was all set to go ahead but two weeks later Eamonn Andrews died and again the idea had to be shelved. It was finally resurrected in the reign of Eamonn's successor, Michael Aspel.

Harry said: "Apparently the name of Sooty cropped up at a planning meeting for *This Is Your Life*. They all thought I'd been done before until someone put them right. So they eventually got round to featuring me, which meant that Marjorie had to keep quiet about it for a whole year. Actually, that wasn't as difficult as it sounds since they used Matthew as their major point of liaison. Matthew was very keen to get me up to the Mayfair Theatre to see his Christmas show so we tentatively arranged for me to come up on Wednesday, 7 December. At one point I wanted to change the date.

"'You can't,' said Matthew.

"'Why not? What's so special about that day?'

"'I want to take you out for a meal afterwards and I've made arrangements so will you please stick to 7 December?'

"'OK, if that's what you want.'

"After we'd travelled up, Matthew asked me: 'Will you change for dinner before the show so we can go out straight afterwards?'

"I thought: 'That's funny. The show ends at

six and you don't normally go out to dinner at that time in London.'

"And he added:'Don't worry if you see Thames Television technicians fixing up lights, they're doing a video for an insert into a later show.'

"All these odd things now began to register. I thought they were going to do an insert of me so when Matthew called me up on stage, I was quite expecting it. What I didn't expect was for this bloody big bear to come on with Michael Aspel inside and announce:'Tonight, Harry Corbett, O.B.E. , This Is Your Life.'"

Once Aspel had extricated himself from his giant Sooty costume, he introduced the likes of Charlie Drake, Steve Race and Gerry Marsden as well as family and old friends such as Reg Dale, Harry's teacher at Carlton High School, Bradford all those years ago. And there was a heart-warming film clip from Fountaindale School in Mansfield where Matthew has continued Harry's tradition of doing a Christmas show for the physically handicapped children. But of course there was only one way the programme could end and that was with Aspel receiving the time-honoured squirt from Sooty's water-pistol.

Harry enjoyed his evening immensely — with one reservation. "I didn't much care for the way in which everyone was given lines to say. Marjorie was told to say certain things about Sooty, like how he acquired his name, which were basically inaccurate. When I guested on Peter Butterworth's *This Is Your Life* many years ago, I wasn't given lines. And if I had been, there's no way I would have stuck to them."

This Is Your Life provided a thoroughly-deserved night of recognition for a man who maybe hasn't always earned the plaudits that his phenomenal achievements have merited. This was partly due to Harry himself. "Matthew loves the limelight," said Harry, "but by nature I'm shy. For me Sooty was always the star. I dread making speeches, I much prefer to keep a low profile. In fact, I won't do a speech unless I've got Sooty with me because then I know the attention will be on him and not me. Sooty is something for me to hide behind. You see, I wasn't born into showbusiness — if Sooty had never happened, I would have been perfectly happy as an electrical engineer."

This goes some way to explaining why Harry never made as much money as he should have out of Sooty. At a time when Phillip Schofield, co-presenter of the Saturday morning children's show *Going Live*, is reported to be well on the way to achieving millionaire status mainly due to his glove puppet Gordon the Gofer, it somehow seems unfair that the inventor of the most enduring children's favourite of all should have had to worry about whether or not he could afford a plush new car.

"I know I should have made more financially," Harry admitted last June. "By rights, I should be a millionaire but I made a few mistakes along the way. The toy shop in Bradford didn't work out and I didn't fare too well out of the Disney deal either. I should have been pushier, but I'm not really made that way. In all that time with the BBC, I never really asked them for a pay rise, I just accepted what they offered. I was definitely a bit slow on that side. Then when Matthew took over, he virtually doubled my salary. But he's tougher, a real businessman. I was happy just to be doing Sooty."

Marjorie adds: "Matthew does it for the money, Harry did it for love. When we were touring, we worked seven days a week for ten years but we never thought of it as work. We'd have done it for nothing."

"There are certain things we can't afford," continued Harry, "like foreign cruises. And I nearly have a fit when I go to the travel agents. But in spite of that, we've managed to get away a few times every year. I suppose not making more money is one thing I'm a bit sad about — but not too much. After all, we're still comfortable."

174

Matthew confirms: "Pop did play it badly, not with regard to Sooty but with bricks and mortar. He didn't move wisely with property — he was not very good at investing the money he had made. He could have moved to a bigger house at a very early stage but instead he stayed at Guiseley. Here was this incredibly famous man with a Rolls-Royce living in a semi-detached house. Having said that, when you look back on the original 7s6d outlay for Sooty, I think it's fair to say we've got our money back."

So how much is Sooty worth today? "In terms of annual turnover," says Matthew, "it has to be millions if you start in Taiwan with the woman who orders the yellow dye for making the puppets. But I only see a small fraction of that because the Sooty empire is a vast pie with a hell of a lot of fingers in it."

One way in which Harry could have made money was from the store of old Sooty tapes that he had kept from the glorious black and white days. The BBC wanted to issue them on video like the *Watch With Mother* collection which, since its release in 1987, has sold over three hundred and fifty thousand copies and shot to number one in the video charts. Spotty Dog lives again! "My Sooty programmes are worth a fortune," said Harry, "but I can't do anything with them because Matthew has the complete copyright and he's issuing his own up-to-date ones. It's a shame, but I can understand his position. It would look odd if the two were put out at the same time and anyway we'd end up cutting each other's throats."

Did Harry have any other regrets? "My one ambition was to get Sooty international, but I'm delighted to say Matthew's a good way to achieving that particular goal. My only real opportunity was when I did those films for Disney. I've never even seen any of them myself but we had to make them in such a hurry that I'm sure they were pretty rough. And I wouldn't have liked to have lived in America — it would have killed me years ago. Besides, we've had a lovely life here.

175

"The other thing that used to niggle me was the merchandising. I know the feeling has always been that Sooty would have a longer life if we didn't overdo it and basically I agree with that but to my mind there simply hasn't been enough merchandising. I've often come away furious that I couldn't find Sooty in the shops. People would say to me: 'Why can't we buy any Sooty or Sweep puppets?' It's so annoying when there are millions of children who think the same about Sooty as their parents did. And I regularly have battles with shopowners who keep their Sooty blind boxes tucked away where hardly anybody can see them. I make them put the boxes on the counter where they're supposed to be. What's the point in having them otherwise? I don't think my action does any good though because I've returned to shops the following day and found that the Sooty box has reverted to its old hidden spot. The boxes raise an enormous amount of money anyway but with a bit of thought from shopkeepers they could do even better."

Harry also still bore a mild grudge at being snubbed by Frank Sinatra over thirty years ago when Ole Blue Eyes was organising a huge show in America in aid of the Save the Children Fund. "I wrote to him saying: 'You're widely regarded as being the best singer in the world, well most people consider me to be the best children's entertainer in the world. I would be more than happy to come and join you on the show.' I waited and waited but never received even so much as a reply. Marjorie says Sinatra doesn't know what he was missing.

Something that Harry missed was his charity work for the National Children's Home. He had devoted an enormous amount of time and energy to the NCH in the Fifties and Sixties, in the process raising a lot of money for them. He simply loved helping children. After raising £504 (which was a sizeable sum in those days) doing a show on the Isle of Man, Harry discovered that the children in the local home didn't have a television set. So on the spot he wrote out a cheque for them to buy one. But sadly after ten years of racing around the country, his increased work-load made it more difficult to fit in shows for the NCH. "Even after my heart attack, I tried to revive my links with them down here in Dorset," said Harry, "but for some reason they didn't really seem interested any more. It was a shame because those shows gave me a great deal of pleasure."

On the other hand, an aspect of his life from which he continued to derive immense satisfaction was that Sooty has remained a family business. Apart from the obvious contributions of Matthew and Marjorie, Leslie and David have also been involved occasionally in recent years. Back in 1987, Harry asked Les to tape the voice of his old pal Ramsbottom the Yorkshire snake for a stage show. Les, who still lives in Guiseley, got a real kick out of it and although the parting was harrowing at the time, he can now also look back fondly on his days with Sweep and he delights in entertaining his grandchildren with the puppets. In the old days, Les was always known as Sooty's uncle, a reminder that Sooty had a very strict family tree which had to be adhered to. For example, Harry detested being called "Sooty's grandad". In his world, both he and Matthew were Sooty's daddy. Poor Les isn't always associated with Sooty at all though. "Unfortunately," he says, "because of my short stature, people tend not to link my surname with Harry — they think I'm the brother of Ronnie Corbett!"

Matthew's brother David was a deputy headmaster at a school in the West Midlands for thirteen years but still found time to help with Sooty's music recording sessions. Harry was very proud to relate that David is now running his own music workshop, at the same time reflecting that he could also have made an impact in showbusiness. "He was a tremendous stage manager and would have made a first-rate producer," said Harry. "One of my greatest thrills is that I've managed to involve all the family in Sooty. I'm so glad it's stayed a family concern. It was so fortunate that Matthew was able to take over, although sometimes I think the puppets are so lifelike they can do the show themselves without any help from humans.

"For years Marjorie and I used to talk about the possibility of retiring. In fact it was our main topic of conversation. But I found I just couldn't stop. Muriel, my sister-in-law, said to me only last year:

"'Harry, you said you would retire at seventy but you're still carrying on. Don't you think you should ease off a bit? Aren't you ever going to retire?'

"I grinned at her. 'I can't Mu, I just can't. I can't let go.'

"The thing is I love entertaining children. Even if I couldn't do it semi-professionally, I'd still do it for charity. I don't think there will ever be a time in my life when I can take Sooty off and say: 'That is the last time I'm going to do it.' I don't think I could ever do that. The thought of losing Sooty for good made me realise that I can't live without him — he's brought so much happiness to us."

Relaxing in his favourite armchair on a warm summer's afternoon, Harry continued: "I can honestly say that despite the bad health we've both suffered along the way, Marjorie and I have had a wonderful time together. Really we've lived two lives in the space of one. We've done so much. I just can't believe all the amazing things that have happened to us. Sometimes I have to pinch myself to make sure it's all real. Every time I wake up, I'm surprised. So after all that we've achieved, I suppose I consider that everything we do from now on is a bonus."

Less than two months after our conversation, Harry Corbett was dead. He went the way he had always wanted to go, shortly after doing a sell-out show with Sooty. On Tuesday, 15 August, Harry and Marjorie had played to a packed audience at Weymouth Pavilion as part of their eight-week summer season. Marjorie recalls: "The audience were particularly marvellous that afternoon and they gave Harry a tumultuous round of applause at the end. He was absolutely thrilled. The following day was a rest day and I remember watching him go out to his workshop and noticing how very low his shoulders looked. I thought: 'Oh, lovey, you do look old.'

"Harry always gave me a goodnight kiss and went to bed before me. I don't know why but that night he came downstairs again, gave me a big hug and another kiss and said: 'I do love you so much.'

"I went upstairs about an hour later. We were supposed to be working the next day so in the morning I touched Harry's arm to wake him up. I immediately thought how cold it was. I rushed round the bed, I didn't dare look at his face, and felt his whole arm. I thought: 'Oh no, he's dead.'

"On reflection, I think he may even have been dead when I got into bed the previous night because there wasn't a ripple in the sheets in the morning. I think he'd just made himself comfortable and died peacefully. What a lovely way to go. I think he must have known he was going to die that night."

Harry Corbett passed away in the early hours of Thursday, 17 August, 1989, aged seventy-one.

The immediate problem was notifying their sons, both of whom were away on holiday. David was camping in the west country while Matthew was staying in his Spanish villa. The Friday before his father's death, Matthew had told me how much he and Sallie were looking forward to the holiday. It had been a hectic year and the moment the break was over, Matthew would have to start preparing for the British and Australian tours. They needed a good rest. And they succeeded in cutting themselves off from the outside world to such an extent that ironically the authorities had tremendous difficulty informing them of Harry's death. Interpol were called in to track him down. Eventually he was found, albeit in an unlikely way.

Matthew says: "We had been in Alicante for four days. It was glorious, there was no rushing around, we were drinking away to our heart's content and the sun was shining. It was perfect relaxation. Then suddenly a man staggered across a building site waving his arms to tell us that my father had died in England. Sallie and I looked at each other. In the past, many people had said, 'Sorry about your father dying' and it had either been Harry H. Corbett of Steptoe fame who died in 1982 or they thought my father had died after his heart attack in the Seventies. So for half-an-hour there was a faint hope that this was another false alarm and that the news wasn't true. Then Sallie rang her mother in England who immediately said: 'Thank God you've phoned, everyone's been looking for you.' And she confirmed our worst fears.

"It was pure chance that we heard about it in the first place. A property agent in Spain who we knew had been driving a couple from the airport to their villa and while they were travelling along in the car, merely to make conversation, he said:

"'I've just had lunch with Matthew Corbett who does Sooty.'

"The couple, who had just arrived from England, replied: 'Oh yes, his father has died. Everybody's looking for him.'

"'My God! He doesn't know. He only lives round the corner, I must tell him.'"

Family and friends flocked to the funeral in Poole, Dorset, but there was one notable absentee — Sooty. Matthew explains: "Sooty only goes to happy events and anyway my dad was the star of that particular show." However at the World and Sooty Museum in Shipley, Harry was remembered in the shape of a floral Sooty made out of yellow chrysanthemums and at the cottage at Child Okeford, David Corbett neatly laid Sooty, Sweep and Soo on Harry's pillow as a mark of respect. At the funeral, Matthew's wreath read: "Dear Pop, Goodbye — I always did and I always will love you." And Marjorie's bore the simple message: "We loved each other so much." Even on such a sad occasion, there was still room for a moment of unintentional humour. Waiting for the appointed time, the funeral director looked at his watch and, with an unfortunate choice of words, announced: "Right, I make it dead on!" Matthew reckons his father would have enjoyed that.

The tributes poured in, although Harry's demise attracted a relatively small amount of television and press coverage. For someone who had created a British institution, Harry received scant recognition whereas soap stars who have done nothing more than recite somebody else's lines (usually badly) frequently command a five-minute spot on the main news and a re-run of their finest hour if they ever had one. The BBC did concede: "Harry Corbett quickly established himself as one of the country's best-loved children's entertainers" but perhaps the most amazing tribute came from Jimmy Savile who generously offered: "Harry was a gentleman and a master of his craft. When he was on *Jim'll Fix It*, I liked him immediately."

"This was remarkable," says Matthew, "because to my knowledge, my father never met Jimmy Savile. He certainly didn't appear on *Jim'll Fix It* — I did!"

Harry's former secretary, Joyce Rumsey, remembers him with great fondness. She says: "I still miss his delightful chuckle and his wonderful sense of humour. I can honestly say we didn't have a cross word in twenty-five years."

Vincent Shaw, his agent for many years, adds: "Harry was a very simple, very happy, ordinary man. He never had a star complex. And every day was a surprise and a delight to him."

Peter Barker, Harry's old commercial agent, recalls Harry's love of children. "He became a great friend of ours and I remember saying to him once: 'Wouldn't it be marvellous if Sooty could appear at my children's birthday party?' My son Charles was three then, it was in about 1960, and my daughter Caroline was six and they were both tremendous Sooty fans. We had organised the party for two hundred children in Mayfair on a December afternoon but unfortunately the previous evening, Harry had been doing a show in Buxton, Derbyshire, which was notorious for being cut off by bad weather. He said he'd do his best to get down to London but he couldn't promise anything. Needless to say, it was thick snow that day and as the party progressed, we still hadn't heard from Harry. We thought: 'That's that then. He'll never make it in this weather.' We had exhausted all the games of musical chairs and the kids were reaching that restive stage at parties where small fights begin to break out when suddenly this snowman appeared at the door. It was Harry, who had somehow managed to drive down and was covered in snow just through walking from his car. He and Sooty entertained the children for a magical half an hour and he still had to drive back up to Buxton the following morning."

Marjorie confirms that Harry was one of the few children's entertainers who actually liked children. "He was so very genuine and he adored children, not like one performer we knew in Guiseley who would think nothing of marching out into the audience and walloping the kids if they got too noisy! We had such a wonderful life together and he was such a kind man — they don't make them like that very often. And it all ended on such a high note although as far as I'm concerned, he's still here with me. You know, right up to the end I watched every performance Harry did. I lived the show even when I wasn't operating Soo and I still got a kick out of it. When Harry put Sooty on, I never thought, 'Oh Christ, he's off again.' Sooty was our life."

Unfortunately, some of the press coverage of Harry's death once again dredged up the long-forgotten "rift" between he and Matthew. It was stated that they were still at loggerheads and had hardly spoken to one another for years. As Matthew has discovered, once your file is labelled 'didn't get on with father', it is extremely difficult to erase. But despite a few disagreements in the take-over days, they actually got on remarkably well in circumstances that weren't always conducive to peace and harmony. For Harry had set extremely high standards with Sooty and Matthew had to live up to them in his eyes. Matthew accepted the challenge and succeeded where many might have expected him to fail. And because Harry was happy with the way Sooty was going, he was happy with Matthew. "In fact, people used to remark about how well we got on for father and son," says Matthew. "Sure we had our altercations but I loved that bugger.

"As far as I'm concerned, he was always the guv'nor. I may be better at quipping and ad-libbing with the audience than he was but he could always perform the magic better than me. He was incredibly talented, far more than I am, and his dexterity just put me to shame. He was thrilled about the way Sooty had progressed. He was a man who had a lucky life and died absolutely content because everything he had always wanted to see happen to Sooty was coming into being, like the increase in merchandising and Sooty going international. One of his great achievements that should not be overlooked was that he did something that very few people manage — he left something in the English language, the phrase 'Izzy Whizzy, Let's Get Busy'. Nowadays if a child wants a toy and the parent asks, 'What are the magic words?' instead of 'please', the kid says 'Izzy Whizzy, Let's Get Busy'. And that item of vocabulary is all due to my father. He also left the Corbett family with the capability to carry on without too much sadness. My mother, even though she doesn't enjoy the best of health herself, was incredibly strong after he died. She almost seemed to find a new inner strength. But that's the way my father would have wanted it — he liked people to get on with life, not sit around moping.

"After he died, many people sent me letters saying how sorry they were. It was very nice to hear that but at the same time I don't feel too sad about the whole thing. After all, he was a very happy man who achieved all he wanted to in life. So nobody should feel sad either for my father or me."

It could also be argued that the Corbetts were able to come to terms with their grief because they had practically been through it all before when Harry had his heart attack. He was not expected to live then, so in showbusiness parlance that served as a "dress rehearsal" for the real thing. In addition, he was only given a maximum of fifteen years to live in 1976 so as he joked to me shortly before his death, "I'm almost past my sell-by date." One thing Marjorie did have to do though was sell Harry's faithful piano to Steinway. She said: "I just couldn't bear the thought of hearing anyone else playing it."

Matthew thinks Harry is still keeping a watchful eye over Sooty anyway. "He always rang me up after the first show of each series to say how much he enjoyed it. I don't know whether he did or not but it was something he did as a loving father. The most recent series began in September, just three weeks after his death, and at the end of the programme, at exactly the time he used to call, the phone rang. I answered it but nobody spoke. . . the line just went dead. I thought: 'I wonder if he's up there trying to call me.' It was really spooky.

"I'll make sure that my father is never forgotten where Sooty is concerned. His voice still introduces the stage show and I go out of my way to include some of his gentler routines. For example, we bake a cake just the way he used to in the Fifties. Two weeks before he died, he finished building that fantastic rocket ship — in fact, he used to tell me that he couldn't pop off until it was completed. What I didn't notice until after his death was that he had put a small plaque on it, inscribed 'made by Harry Corbett'. It makes you wonder whether he knew that it would be the last thing he would make. We used the rocket set as the basis for stage shows here and in Australia and whenever I told the audience that it had been built by my late father over a period of two years, it always brought a nice round of applause. It was an exceedingly complicated piece of equipment and I think my father would have chuckled at what happened to me on about the third occasion I used it.

"There are levers on the rocket ship to lift and lower Sooty so when the children shout, 'He's there', I pull the lever, he disappears and I say, 'I can't see him.' And then using another Sooty and another lever, I make him appear somewhere else. So it looks as if he's flitting about all over the ship. After a couple of days of working the apparatus successfully, I thought I'd mastered it and got a bit over-confident. I tried to work the mechanism really quickly but I went too far and it all became twisted. I knew by the audience's reaction that something was wrong and after a minute of confusion, I looked down to find a Sooty below me and another one by my left ear. So the audience could see two Sootys. I had to think on my feet and said: 'Sooty, how many times have I told you not to invite your twin brother on stage?' It got me out of having to explain to the kids how there could be two Sootys and earned appreciation from the adults who knew that I'd made a mistake. But I could just hear my father laughing and telling me: 'That'll teach you to be too cocky.'"

But what of Sooty? What are his chances of carrying on for another forty years now that his original "daddy" is no longer around? "Sooty is currently going through a very good period," says Matthew. "My audience keeps regenerating. At the same time as some teenagers decide they've grown out of Sooty, a whole new crop of toddlers come along as new viewers. It's one big cycle. And the various areas of activity are now strong and healthy. I wasn't as optimistic three years ago though. I had received a tax bill for £35,000 due to an accountants' error and not unreasonably I decided to employ somebody else to handle my financial affairs in future. I explained to my new accountant exactly what my job was and said to him: 'This is not a business I see as growing. As a matter of fact, I think I'm going to see a gradual decrease in the income from it. I feel the peak has been passed.' But since then, there has been such a massive upward turn, it's unbelievable. Part of the problem was that at that time there was a significant dip in the number of children who were at the right age to watch Sooty. Four years ago, I was playing to ten per cent fewer children than when my father was in charge or even when I first started. This was because there was a sudden population drop — for some reason fewer babies were being born. Consequently, sales of Sooty merchandising weren't growing, they were just standing still. But now I'm pleased to say we're coming out of that period."

Things are really looking up for Sooty. In recent years, his profile has remained decidedly low in comparison to the likes of Thomas the Tank Engine but in the second half of 1989 two major new developments have put him right back in the limelight. One has been his return to the world of commercials. Some thirty-three years after winning the international award for his Oxo advert, Sooty has made a screen comeback by promoting the Rafford Fireplace. "Although the IBA won't permit us to endorse children's products," says Matthew, "there is nothing to stop us doing adult commercials. This fireplace was invented by a Russian count and its great advantage is that it burns without a flue. So the agency given the task of thinking up an advertising campaign for it were pondering: 'There's no soot and you don't need a sweep. . . How about Sooty and Sweep?' The good thing is that most of the advertising men nowadays are about nineteen which means they remember me from the days when they watched Sooty as kids. I'm getting older but admen are getting younger.

They're Sooty people which is terrific because it could open up whole new areas for us."

The other area of expansion has been into educational videos. In September 1989, Thames Video Collection and Video Collection International released a series of four Sooty educational videos, entitled *Learn With Sooty*. Aimed at two to seven year-olds, they cover reading, numbers, science and safety (which includes hazards like sharp knives, electricity and sensitive areas such as dealing with strangers). All are presented in such a way as to show youngsters that learning can be fun. Over one hundred and twenty thousand copies were pre-sold and within a month all four films had entered Woolworth's top twenty video chart.

The idea to make them stemmed partly from the IBA's comments to Matthew about Sooty's enormous influence over the minds of young children and partly from the letters he receives from parents. Matthew says: "We've moved into areas I never thought we'd get to with Sooty and these educational videos are an example of that. A lot of mums used to say to me: 'I've got a bone to pick with you. I have to watch your Sooty video every morning at seven before my daughter goes to school and the moment she gets home from school she wants it on again. If I see that video again, I'll go stark raving mad.' Many, many people have told me that because it seems that children like repetition. So I thought if they like an ordinary Sooty programme video to be repeated, how much better if they watch something that's actually teaching them at the same time. So we made the educational videos. Also, if the IBA are right about how powerful Sooty is, that children take an avid interest in the way he acts and the subjects he discusses, then an awful lot of children are going to learn an awful lot of information from these videos. And that can't be a bad thing.

"They are selling so well that the people behind them are already talking about making more. They say the next one should be *Sooty Goes Green* because although he's yellow, he does care about green issues." So it looks as if Sooty will become an environment-friendly bear. And until now he probably thought the Greenhouse Effect was something that happened to Bill and Ben.

It was also a wise move to involve Thames Television in the making of the videos. In the face of increased competition from satellite channels and with a quarter of production now having to be made by independent companies, these are harrowing times for television in general but for ITV in particular. For in addition the government proposes to auction ITV franchises off to the highest bidder when they come up for renewal in 1992. So after the glory years of the Seventies, it is a time of financial restraint with many programmes either operating on reduced budgets or being axed altogether. Unfortunately the least economic programmes to make are children's shows so if money is tight, these are the first to suffer. Thames and other ITV companies had already announced that they were cutting down on the number of children's programmes to be made in the future (the shift is towards cheaper cartoons made by small independent companies) and there was a fear that Sooty, at £750,000 a series, could become a casualty. So Vincent Shaw, Sooty's guardian angel, decided to include Thames in the educational video project on the basis that if they had a financial interest in Sooty, they would be less likely to drop the programme.

Matthew is so concerned about the effect that the deregulation of television might have on Sooty and indeed children's programming in general that he has joined a campaign called BAC TV (British Action for Children's Television) to try and fight the proposals. Many of the country's leading producers of children's programmes are lending their support to the movement. They believe that what youngsters watch is of vital importance and while they are realistic enough to acknowledge that they have little hope of persuading the government to drop deregulation altogether, they want to ensure that firm controls remain so that the quality of children's television is maintained. It is their opinion that children deserve variety and diversity in their viewing, not just a stream of cartoons. One of BAC TV's prime movers is actor Tony Robinson, a highly-inventive maker of children's shows such as last year's off-beat Robin Hood spoof *Maid Marian and Her Merry Men,* but best known as the brain-dead Baldrick in *Blackadder.* Co-incidentally he was in the year above Matthew at drama school. So when Matthew heard about this campaign, he phoned Tony Robinson and said: "I'm the nauseating youth who was in the year below you at college. What can I do to help?"

Another way of safeguarding Sooty's future is to develop him as a character. This the aim of Pat Redmond of Patsy B. Marketing who for the past two years have been in charge of Sooty's commercial side. "Sooty is famous but commercially undeveloped," says Pat. "The commercial activity was there many years ago but it then disappeared. Yet remarkably although all the products went, the character of Sooty carried on regardless. But now there is a great deal of activity again. Commercially, nothing stands out like reputation and Sooty has a great reputation. But the character must continue to grow. It is really a question of putting a modern interpretation on Sooty, bringing the old up to date in the way that Disney have done. We couldn't have left it the way it was, we've had to bring out a whole new range of products. The old Sooties are so quaint they're in the Sooty Exhibition at the museum in Shipley. The exhibition itself is another possible area of progress. We've already had enquiries from Australia, Hong Kong, Japan and many places in Britain to make it a travelling exhibition. It would cost £250,000 to put it on the road but if it goes ahead, it would be a big development for Sooty. I'd like to think Sooty could go into Europe too. After all, Lego are a Danish company and they have a tour in this country. Well we'd like to do it the other way round. It all adds up to a very exciting time as we gear ourselves towards his fortieth anniversary on TV in 1992."

Just as Sooty is planning to expand overseas, his Christmas show in London is also moving to larger premises. The record-breaking run at the Mayfair is over. Christmas 1989 was his last show there. The theatre is becoming a conference centre so from this winter Sooty is switching to the Bloomsbury which, with five hundred and sixty seats, has more than twice the capacity of the Mayfair.

But the shock news for Sooty fans is that Matthew plans to retire in eight years time when he's fifty. "A few years ago, Sallie and I went through a bit of a rough patch as do most marriages at one stage or another. When we'd resolved our problems, I felt so good about it that I began to look at places where we could retire. At the same time I said: 'I'm going to stop smoking.' And I did. I thought that everything was going so well in my life that it would be just my luck to get stricken with cancer.

"Sallie worries about me. She says I don't smile as much as I used to, although in myself I feel extremely optimistic. She's also trying to stop me working so hard." Just six days before Harry's death, Matthew added poignantly: "She reminds me of the effect all those years of relentless drive and hard work with Sooty had on my father. So I've promised Sallie that I'll review myself and Sooty when I'm fifty, before I have a heart attack like my father. I'm trying to cut back a little anyway because what's the use of retiring at fifty, only to die from a heart attack at fifty-four?

"So that's what I intend to do. I'm certainly not retiring because I'm rich. I'm no millionaire. I accept that we should be wealthier and sometimes I'm puzzled as to why others appear to have more money than us. I've got a job where I consider myself to be fairly well paid, yet all around me I see people who aren't celebrities with far bigger houses and more expensive cars. And I wonder what they must do for a living. Having said that, I've got all I want really. We've got a nice house complete with a multi-track recording studio where I write and record the music for the stage shows, and in some respects I've got more than many wealthy people. I'm thinking of the Jerry Halls and George Harrisons of this world who are so famous that they find it difficult to step out of the front door and are almost prisoners of their own success. At least I'm not that well-known that I can't go to the local Chinese restaurant, although school fetes can sometimes be a bit tricky. By the time I'm fifty, the children will probably have left home so we can settle for a smaller house in this country, together with a boat for touring canals and a place in Spain."

Vincent Shaw believes he has already detected a change in Matthew following the death of his father. "Matthew is a slightly different person since Harry died. He's now his own man — it's as if he's no longer got a ghost on his shoulder."

So what will become of Sooty after his and Matthew's fiftieth birthday in 1998? Will he drift away to a club for retired puppets where he can sit around all day and swap showbiz anecdotes with Rag, Tag and Bobtail and Bill and Ben, talk about Little Weed behind her stem and make absolutely sure that Spit the Dog is blackballed for membership?

"Maybe one of my own children will end up doing Sooty," says Matthew. "They say they won't but they may — after all, at their age I was adamant that I would never take over. Even if they don't, there are still various options open to him — who knows, he could well become a cartoon character. Obviously at this stage it's impossible to say exactly what will happen to him but I'm certain he'll survive somehow, somewhere. Sooty will never, ever die."

It is indeed reassuring news to know that Sooty is immortal. Children and adults alike will now be able to sleep soundly in their beds at night. The pound will probably rise three points against the deutschmark. And all because a humble Bradford engineer stumbled across a novelty shop on Blackpool pier forty-two years ago.

Perhaps Harry Corbett's career is best summed up by the person who was his staunchest supporter throughout, his widow Marjorie. She once offered this profound judgment on her husband's chosen lifestyle: "Harry is the only man I know who can stick his hand up a bear's backside, wiggle its ears and make money." But that's no ordinary bear, that's Sooty.